Living in
Gratitude

Living in Gratitude

Mastering the Art of
Giving Thanks Every Day,
A Month-by-Month Guide

Angeles Arrien

SOUNDS TRUE
Boulder, Colorado

Sounds True, Inc.
Boulder, CO 80306

© 2011, 2013 Angeles Arrien
© 2011, 2013 Foreword by Marianne Williamson

Published 2013

Acknowledgments and Permissions: The author and publisher gratefully acknowledge permission to use quotations from the works of authors listed here. Every effort has been made to clear reprints, and in a few instances, permission was not received in time for formal acknowledgement. If any required credits have been omitted or any rights overlooked, it is completely unintentional, and we will gladly correct any omissions in future reprints.

Cover design by Levi Stephen
Book design by Dean Olson
Printed in the United States of America

Library of Congress Cataloging-in-Publication

Arrien, Angeles, 1940-
   Living in gratitude : mastering the art of giving thanks every day : a month-by-month guide / Angeles Arrien.
      pages cm
Includes bibliographical references.
ISBN 978-1-60407-984-5
1. Gratitude. 2. Conduct of life. I. Title.
BJ1533.G8A77 2013
179'.9--dc23
                                    2013015308
ISBN 978-1-60407-984-5
Ebook ISBN 978-1-60407-641-7
10 9 8 7 6 5 4 3

For all my Basque Ancestors

and especially for my grandparents:

Lorenzo and Juana

and

Calixto and Petra

Contents

Acknowledgments xix

Foreword by Marianne Williamson xxiii

Introduction 1

1. January: Begin Anew 23

*Four Concerns of Soul Making • Hopi Reminders
for Starting Anew • Renewed Innocence:
Five Qualities of Children*

2. February: Attend to the Heart 41

*The Four-Chambered Heart • Spoken and Non-spoken
Verses of Love • Dalai Lama's Practice of Cherishing
Self and Others*

3. March: Compassionate Service 61

*Five Principles of Compassionate Service •
Luck: Where Opportunity and Preparedness Intersect •
Nabokov's "Thrill of Gratitude"*

Contents

4. April: Mercy and Atonement 77

*Spirituality of Empathy • States of Ingratitude •
The Cultivation of Mercy and Forgiveness*

5. May: The Gift of Grace 95

*Grace, Gravitas, and Gratitude • Memorial Day
and Aboriginal Dreamtime • Nine Practices of
Excellence from Japan*

6. June: The Power of Equanimity 115

*Balance, Equanimity, and Renewal • Japanese
Practice of Naikan • The Practice and Identification
of Equanimity*

7. July: Embracing Nature 131

*Four Natural Qualities for Survival • Nature's
Three Laws of Governance • Four Soul Retrieval
Places in Nature*

8. August: Cultivating Peace 149

*Embracing Nonviolence: The Quaker Queries •
Shifting Our Relationship to Conflict: Questions from
the Talmud • Three Guidelines for Fair Fighting*

9. September: Opening to Guidance and Wisdom . . 167

*Seven Outer Practices of Highly Effective People •
Seven Internal Practices for Developing Spirituality
and Character • Five Principles of Optimum Health*

Contents

10. October: Letting Be and Letting Go 185

*Deeper Lessons of Living and Being Human •
Longings and Belongings • Community and
Celebration: Being a Social Architect*

11. November: Grateful Seeing 203

*The Breath of Thanks Practice • Indigenous
Giveaway Practices • Grateful Seeing: Looking
for Goodness and What Is Working*

12. December: The Mystic Heart 221

*The Holidays and the Mystic Heart • Two Kinds
of Gratitude • Gift-Giving and Royal Generosity*

Epilogue: Living in Gratitude — Where We
Have Been and How We Can Continue 237

Notes 241

Bibliography 251

Reader's Guide 267

About the Author 273

Acknowledgments

I AM FOREVER grateful for all the people and circumstances who have and continue to fill my life with blessings,
learnings, mercies, and protections, and especially:

- For the gift of life itself, and the Great Mystery of how it
continues to unfold.

- For the gift of family and those loved ones who have
become extended family, all of whom continue to teach
me about the importance of love, loyalty, authenticity,
and generosity of spirit—especially my sister Joanne, who
best embodies these qualities, and who is my greatest
friend and ally. She is the one person who has and
continues to be there for me, no matter what.

- For the gift of friendship, and for all those who continue
to offer that precious experience to me—especially those
whom I have known for fifteen to forty-five years. You
know who you are.

- For the gift of collegiality shared with my colleagues. You
all inspire me and continue to create many opportunities

and challenges so that my creative gifts can be utilized and expressed more fully in each decade of my life.

- For the gift of teaching and learning, especially for all the students, participants, organizations, and institutions that continue to be drawn to my seminars, classes, workshops, and consulting services. You all help me actualize my life dream and purpose, for which I am forever grateful.

- For the great gift of faith, and the solace and sanctuary it always provides.

- And last, but not least, for the gift of the angels, the visible and invisible ones, who helped me manifest this book.

To those who have pioneered and expanded the field of gratitude, particularly Brother David Steindl-Rast, M. J. Ryan, and Sarah Ban Breathnach and researchers Robert Emmons, Michael McCullough, Johanna Hill, Barbara Fredrickson, and Martin Seligman, whose work has inspired me to write this book. It is important to acknowledge that the work of gratitude is an expansion of what began in the field of humanistic psychology with Abraham Maslow's pioneering work. This work later influenced the development of transpersonal psychology and consciousness studies, which was pioneered by Tony Sutich, Sonya Margulies, Miles Vich, James Fadiman, Bob Frager, Stan and Christina Grof, Frances Vaughan, Roger Walsh, Charles Tart, and Arthur Hastings. Abundant gratitude to anthropologists Mircea Eliade, Margaret Mead, Sandra and Michael Harner, and Alan Dundes, whose work

Acknowledgments

has stimulated and influenced my interests in cross-cultural and perennial wisdom. I am also deeply grateful to the work of Joseph Campbell and Huston Smith, both of whom have shaped my continued interest in mythology, symbology, comparative religions, and interfaith work. And with deep appreciation to the Fetzer Institute and its visionary founder, John E. Fetzer.

Many thanks to all those from Sounds True who have believed in and worked on this book, especially Tami Simon, Jaime Schwalb, Haven Iverson, and the creative design staff that made this book so beautiful. Gratitude also to editor Sheridan McCarthy, whose efficiency helped me develop, clarify, and format the material into a more accessible form. This is a better book because of her efforts. And special thanks to Marianne Williamson for her inspirational and thoughtful foreword.

Limitless gratitude especially to Tenzin Lhadron, my excellent executive administrator, who not only kept everything going in my Sausalito office, but whose flexibility, focus, patience, insight, competence, quality feedback, and generosity of spirit were invaluable and immeasurable in bringing the manuscript into publishable form; and to her research assistant Ashley Eagle-Gibbs, who helped her with the permissions for this book.

—Angeles Arrien
Sausalito, California

Foreword

GRATITUDE IS ONE of those words that no one disagrees with, as in: "Well, of *course* we should all be grateful. And now pass the salad, please. Nothing more to really discuss about that, is there?"

So it is that we subtly, even insidiously, avoid the tremendous powers of some of our greatest gifts: by simply viewing them as a given. If something's obvious, then why investigate it further? But the obviousness of a concept like, "You should always say thank you," hides an entire world of possibilities. If I give you a drink of water and you say thank you, then I'm more likely to want to give you another one should you become thirsty again. But if I give you a drink of water and you don't have the courtesy to say thank you, then I'm more likely to figure you can get your own darn glass of water next time.

The same is true with the universe—not to anthropomorphize it or ascribe to it the characteristics of a petty ego. It's just that whether we're talking about other people, or the Creator itself, there is something about the expression of gratitude that opens doors that do not otherwise open. This is a spiritual fact.

As Angeles Arrien makes eloquently clear in this lovely treatise on the powers of gratitude, the modern mind is deeply in need of a more contemplative dimension. Blessings, mercy, tenderness, nature, forgiveness, and compassionate relationships exist in our world, yet they compete with the noise and obsessions of video games, computers, greed, and peer pressure. We know we're off balance, yet we often struggle to realign ourselves. Rarely do we realize that if we simply take time to marvel at life's gifts and give thanks for them, we activate stunning opportunities to increase their influence in our lives. Throughout her career, Arrien has been one of our most able guides along the path to restoring and revitalizing our psyche. With this book, she continues to weave her unique and magical spell; she deepens our understanding of words and concepts we already appreciate intellectually but might not feel in our hearts. Through her tutelage, we come to understand these concepts on the level that counts: deep within us.

Simply reading this book is an act of power, as it gently casts superfluous considerations out of your mind and focuses you on things that matter most. You will reengage truths that most of us already know yet keep at an emotional distance. What you knew, but only abstractly, will become knowledge that both informs your soul and transforms your life.

Reading this book and learning from its lessons, you will focus on the blessings and spiritual treasures of life—from the beauty of a bird's song to an act of selfless service. Such things will become as meaningful and as important to you as any material thing you value now. Your mind will strengthen, your heart will soften, your relationship to nature will be enriched, and your own internal landscape will be re-greened. You will see yourself and others in a more beautiful and truthful light. And you will be deeply grateful for all of the above.

In my own path as a seeker and teacher, I have greatly valued the work of Angeles Arrien. Within the pages of *Living in Gratitude,* we receive more of her wise and most excellent guidance, helping us deepen our journeys into the light at the center of who we truly are. And with her presence in our lives, we are blessed.

—Marianne Williamson, author of
The Age of Miracles and *The Gift of Change*

Introduction

*If the only prayer you say in your whole life is
"thank you," that would suffice.*

MEISTER ECKHART

THE APPLICATION OF multicultural wisdom—the
shared values and the inherent positive beliefs of humanity—
has become known as *perennial wisdom*. Perennial wisdom
has been passed on from generation to generation since the
birth of humankind. It continues to surface among diverse
peoples, unconnected by geography or language, yet inextricably linked to what is inherently important in our shared
experience of what it means to be human. Of all the universal themes that have been transmitted through perennial

wisdom, the expression of gratitude continues to be the glue that consistently holds society and relationships together; its opposite—ingratitude—contributes to societal dissolution and separation. The expression of gratitude is essential to humankind's sustainability and survival. Gratitude's stabilizing and healing effects, which have been researched from multiple standpoints—cultural, psychological, physical, spiritual, even financial—have made it abundantly clear that the benefits of living a grateful life are irrefutable.

If gratitude is a state of being that is essential to a life well lived, why then do we not cultivate and express it on a daily basis? After all, giving thanks and expressing appreciation for the blessings and gifts of life is a natural human response. Perhaps the key reason we do not make gratitude a part of our daily lives is that the accelerated pace and multiple distractions of modern life have simply made it all too easy to forget gratitude's importance.

We need not settle for our present disconnection from the healing, life-affirming, and uplifting human experience of gratitude. By engaging with the perennial wisdoms, we are reminded of our natural capacity to feel and express gratitude. Through conscious and sustained practice over a period of time, we can discover again how gratitude and all its related qualities—thankfulness, appreciation, compassion, generosity, grace, and so many other positive states—can become integrated and embodied in our lives. And when people in great numbers choose to practice, integrate, and embody gratitude, the cumulative force that is generated can help create the kind of world we all hope for and desire for ourselves and for future generations.

What Is Gratitude?

Every language in the world has a way of saying "thank you." This is because gratitude is an inherent quality that resides within each human being, and is triggered and expressed spontaneously in a variety of different contexts. Gratitude crosses all boundaries—creed, age, vocation, gender, and nation—and is emphasized by all the great religious traditions.

Gratitude is essentially *the recognition of the unearned increments of value in one's experience*—the acknowledgment of the positive things that come our way that we did not actively work toward or ask for. The *International Encyclopedia of Ethics* defines gratitude as "the heart's internal indicator on which the tally of gifts outweighs exchanges," a definition that echoes the notion of unearned increments. The connection to the concept of gifts is a natural one. The Latin root of the word *gratitude* is *grata* or *gratia*—a given gift—and from this same root we get our word *grace,* which means a gift freely given that is unearned.

Gratitude is a feeling that spontaneously emerges from within. However, it is not simply an emotional response; it is also a choice we make. We can choose to be grateful, or we can choose to be ungrateful—to take our gifts and blessings for granted. As a choice, gratitude is an attitude or disposition. As writer Alexis de Tocqueville once described it, gratitude is "a habit of the heart." Brother David Steindl-Rast, a

Benedictine monk, reminds us that "gratefulness is the inner gesture of *giving* meaning to our life by *receiving* life as gift." M. J. Ryan's classic book *Attitudes of Gratitude* supports the idea that gratitude is a stance we voluntarily take, and one we can adopt through the difficult seasons of life as well as the good ones. The daily practice of gratitude keeps the heart open regardless of what comes our way.

Gratitude as Virtue

Virtues are qualities that support the inherent goodness that resides within each human being. Gratitude is both a social and a theological virtue. The Hebrew scriptures, the New Testament, and the Qur'an all cite gratitude as central among virtues. Centuries ago, the philosopher Cicero argued that gratitude is the parent of all virtues, a virtue that begets other virtues. The cultivation of gratitude develops character, the embodiment of desired virtues. The advice to cultivate character by expanding one's capacity for gratitude is time-honored wisdom. The art of maintaining a grateful disposition engenders other virtues such as generosity, humility, compassion, wisdom, joy, integrity, and trust. This disposition of mindfulness, of being aware of and thankful for our blessings, helps cultivate our virtues and significantly diminishes, or can even eradicate, any obstacles to gratitude we may face.

Related Qualities

There are several words that arise repeatedly when discussing gratitude, all of which reflect states that are related to it.

Introduction

While gratitude is both a feeling and an attitude, *thankfulness* is the demonstrative expression of it, whether extended to ourselves or others. We can express thanks in words—spoken or written—or in deeds, by extending time, resources, or gifts to support people in unexpected ways or to help those in need. *Appreciation* is the recognition of that which makes us feel grateful, and can also be expressed internally or externally. Gratitude often ignites acts of generosity; we are moved to offer ourselves to others without expecting anything in return. Buddhists refer to generous acts that are freely given as "royal generosity." These are just a few of the qualities related to gratitude. The expression of gratitude creates an opening that invites many other positive states and experiences into our lives.

Four Universal Portals to Gratitude: Blessings, Learnings, Mercies, and Protections

There are four portals—or entryways—to the experience of gratitude. Recognizing these portals at the time when they appear in our lives is key to developing the capacity to cultivate gratitude. *Blessings* are the primary, cross-cultural portal through which we experience gratitude. Additionally, *learnings, mercies,* and *protections* are three other portals attributed with fostering gratitude in various worldwide cultures. Each month we will be tracking these portals and how they are surfacing in our work, relationships, health, finances, and personal growth.

Blessings

Blessings are those experiences we hold as "the good" in our lives. The language of blessing is invocation, a calling forth. To bless is to sanctify; to recognize the presence of grace; to confer well-being or prosperity upon others; to endow; or to invoke divine favor upon others or ourselves. Giving gratitude for our blessings is a way to recognize and honor them. John O'Donohue writes in his book *To Bless the Space Between Us*, "The word *blessing* evokes a sense of warmth and protection; it suggests that no life is alone or unreachable. Each life is clothed in raiment of spirit that secretly links it to everything else. Though suffering and chaos befall us, they can never quench that inner light of providence." Blessings are gifts that open doors to healing, connection, meaning, and transformation. Essentially, the world itself cannot exist without blessings.

Learnings

Whenever we are learning, we are growing. Often, what we are learning challenges us to stretch, to reexamine, and to rise to a new standard of excellence or skill level. We do not develop without learning. Our curiosity motivates exploration, risk, and facing the new or unfamiliar—all challenges that lead to learning. The meaning of the word "challenge," from a cross-cultural point of view, is an invitation to grow or extend beyond what is presently knowable or familiar. It is interesting to note that in hindsight, we often refer to our challenges or learnings as blessings in disguise or wake-up calls.

Introduction

We are continually learning about ourselves, each other, our immediate environments, our communities, and the world. "What did I learn today?" is a profound question. It is from our learnings that we are able to bring forward and understand what is meaningful for us. The poet and novelist Marge Piercy sums up the crucible of learning this way: "Life is the first gift, love is the second, and understanding is the third." Our learnings and the understandings we derive from them form a universal portal that engenders gratitude for all the ways we learn, including initiation rituals or rites of passage that occur worldwide.

Mercies

To be merciful is to have a disposition of kindness and compassion that bestows unexpected forgiveness or clemency. Mercy alleviates distress through acts of charity or benevolence. Merciful acts generate thankfulness, both in those who have initiated the acts and those who have benefited from them.

Mercy and forgiveness are closely tied; forgiveness is an act of generosity and compassion that fosters mercy. When we extend acts of kindness and compassion to ourselves and others, we cultivate mercy and open more easily to our own forgiveness work—forgiving ourselves for the harm we have caused and forgiving those who have harmed us. Making amends and extending a genuine apology foster the experience of atonement, "at-one-ment." Anyone who has ever received the gift of forgiveness knows that it is one of the greatest gifts they can receive, and their gratitude emerges spontaneously.

Protections

Inherent in all humans is the instinct to protect ourselves and others, especially those we love—to keep ourselves and others safe from harm, injury, or attack. Every culture has practices, prayers, rituals, and invocations for protection. Housewarmings are blessing and protection rituals, as are ribbon-cutting ceremonies: in cutting the ribbon before walking into a new workplace, we ask for blessings and protections to cut away the old and open to the new. Worldwide, parents bless their children to keep them safe, and remain vigilant in their efforts to keep them from harm. Feeling protected always engenders gratitude, and this is not limited to those who protect us in the seen world such as our elders, or others who may choose to watch out for us. We also call on the help of ancestors, the Mystery, and spiritual figures such as saints and angels for protection.

These universal portals of blessings, learnings, mercies, and protections offer the human spirit the gift of awareness, the ability to recognize all those things that can inspire gratitude amid the paradox of life's happiness and suffering. As Robert Emmons reminds us in his book *Thanks!*, whether we are happy or suffering, "Gratitude is the way the heart remembers—remembers kindnesses, cherished interactions with others, compassionate actions of strangers, surprise gifts, and everyday blessings. By remembering we honor and acknowledge the many ways in which who and what we are has been shaped by others, both living and dead." We can understand the magnitude of gratitude's power when we consider how the intention of thankfulness corresponds with the deepest human realities of connection, creativity, healing, and wholesomeness.

The Benefits of Gratitude in the Four Quadrants of Life

One of the great benefits of a gratitude practice is the ability to track how the four universal portals of gratitude appear in our lives. When we do this, we find that the benefits of gratitude practice are multidimensional. Four quadrants of life experience, which human beings experience cross-culturally, are health and well-being; work environments and communities; financial stability; and relationships. Two other areas of human experience—character development and spiritual growth—are influenced by, and in turn influence, all four quadrants. As a result, gratitude practice in the Four Quadrants of Life also benefits our personal evolution.

Benefits for Health and Well-Being

Our physical state is fertile ground for the four portals to gratitude. We may be thankful that we have learned how to nourish our bodies; that we are protected from once-serious diseases, now eradicated from our modern world; that we have been nursed through an illness with kindness and compassion and that, emerging from this suffering, we are once again blessed with health and well-being.

Dr. Michael McCullough of the University of Miami and Dr. Robert Emmons of the University of California, Davis are among researchers investigating the effects of gratitude practice. Their studies have shown that regularly and deliberately expressing appreciation and genuine thankfulness improves health and well-being. Study participants who kept gratitude journals and practiced self-guided exercises slept better, exercised more, experienced increased positive emotions, progressed toward personal goals more quickly, and helped others more often. In *Words for Gratitude,* Dr. Emmons and Joanna Hill write, "We have learned from research that grateful people elicit more support from others. They cope better, have better health, and are more socially adaptable. This strong data supports grateful behavior. The key is learning how to make it a part of our experience."

Benefits for Work Environments and Communities

Work is what we have come here to do: our contribution to the world, our purpose, our calling. As Kahlil Gibran said, "Work is love made visible." For some people—technology workers, for example—work may involve maintaining and sustaining the systems that lend efficiency to our modern lives. These are the people whose work keeps the world connected and informed. For artists, work means nurturing creativity and inspiration and generating original images, songs, or other objects of beauty. For still others, work is entwined with service; health care professionals and social workers engage in work in this way. We may fit into more than one of these categories simultaneously—doing technical work by day and volunteer work in the evening, for example—or we may fit neatly into one category early in our work life and switch to another at midlife.

Introduction

While our focus may change, one thing does not: the four portals to the experience of gratitude are active within all realms of work. Blessings, learnings, mercies, and protections continually occur in some form or another in all aspects of our working lives.

Both positive and negative emotions have the capacity to affect those around us, often creating a contagious effect. Like many positive emotions such as joy, contentment, inspiration, curiosity, and love, gratitude appears to have the capacity to transform individuals, organizations, and communities for the better. According to Barbara Fredrickson in Emmons and McCullough's book, *The Psychology of Gratitude:*

> It is important to note that positive emotions propagate in groups and communities not simply because smiles are contagious (i.e., through facial mimicry), but because emotions stem from—and create—meaningful interpersonal encounters. When people act on their experiences of gratitude, for instance, they create meaningful situations for others . . . This socioemotional cycle centered on gratitude could continue indefinitely. In this manner, positive emotions tend to beget subsequent positive emotions. Accordingly, the broaden-and-build-theory predicts that positive emotions not only produce individuals who function at higher levels, but also produce organizations and communities that function at higher levels.

Existing research already shows that organizations with employees who experience frequent positive emotions have lower employee turnover, more customer loyalty, higher net sales, and in turn, more profitable financial outcomes.

Benefits for Financial Well-Being

In the financial dimension of our lives, we first strive to be solvent and secure enough to attend to our families. As our finances strengthen, we may widen our circle of support to include extended family or people in need within our communities. The financial quadrant is about our experience of solvency and abundance.

A blessing may come in the form of an unexpected bonus, something we can easily be thankful for. We may come to understand the reason that a certain part of our business is not succeeding—a learning that offers within it the opportunity to shift course and welcome new possibilities such as a different way of doing business. Or we may receive a gift of funds at a time of great need: a manifestation of compassion and mercy. We may seek protection in the very literal form of homeowner's insurance or another kind of insurance policy. When we focus our attention on all of the ways we are supported by our financial life, we find many opportunities to be grateful for what we have.

We know that consistent, meaningful expressions of gratitude by leaders, managers, mentors, and supervisors have the effect of increasing productivity, enhancing creativity, and encouraging cooperation. In environments where workers' value is openly expressed, there is a positive impact on the financial bottom line.

People respond positively to gratitude, and this response directly impacts both people's generosity and their relationship to abundance. A 1976 survey by Carey, Clicque, Leighton, and Milton, published in the *Journal of Marketing*, found that customers of a jewelry store who were called and thanked for coming to the store showed a subsequent 70 percent increase in purchases. In comparison, customers who were called and thanked and told about an upcoming sale showed a 30 percent increase in purchases, and customers who were not called at all did not show any increase. A later study in 1995 by Rind and Bordia found that restaurant patrons gave larger tips when their servers wrote "thank you" on their checks. Gratitude, generosity, and abundance are often braided together within human nature, and when expressed externally produce increase for all.

Benefits for Relationships

Relationships, too, are vessels for the four portals to gratitude. We may receive the blessing of a loving life-partnership; lessons about communicating with greater compassion and integrity; the mercy of a close friend offering kindness; and the protection of a parent. All relationships offer such potential for the experience of gratitude.

The longest relationship we have is with ourselves. Therefore, an important component of our life's experience is to befriend ourselves as we are. Oscar Wilde is reputed to have said, "Be yourself, everyone else is already taken." To befriend ourselves, it is necessary to extend appreciation to ourselves, to at least the same degree we offer it to others.

Emmons and McCullough's research reinforces that gratitude is developed and shaped within interpersonal relationships and social interactions. Gratitude functions in the chain of reciprocity—the give-and-take factor in relationships—which does not incur indebtedness. Put another way, in relationships, gratitude and generosity are intertwined. The capacity to be grateful and generous develops in the context of family and social relationships, and gratitude plays a crucial role in establishing and maintaining all such relations. By mutual giving, people become tied to each other by a web of feelings of gratitude.

Benefits for Character Development and Spiritual Growth

Character development is about the values we hold and the roles we assume as we move through our lives. We move toward development when we are in touch with our authentic voice, our authentic self, and when we are living with integrity and honesty. When we hold opposing qualities within our nature in responsible and balanced ways, we develop personal character and increase our relationship skills. For example, if we can stay in a committed relationship without becoming excessively dependent and remain free without being irresponsible or negligent, we stretch our capacity for developing character; we become more effective in all four aspects of life. As James

Introduction

Hillman wrote in his book *The Force of Character,* "Character begins to govern life's decisions ever more pertinently, and permanently. Values come under more scrutiny, and qualities such as decency and gratitude become more precious than accuracy and efficiency."

Spirituality gives meaning to life, and spiritual growth is about discovering meaning. Spirituality is often expressed in religious terms, but it is the experience of recognizing states of grace, the transcendent, synchronicity, and that which is sacred or holy; it can be found in nature, silence, art, music, family, and friendship. It can bring wholeness to the emotional, physical, and intellectual dimensions of life. The spirit, or life force, within us is the essence or center point of mystery and meaning that is present at the core of our essential nature. It is the force that allows us to integrate our internal and external experiences. The essence of spirituality provides a sense of intactness and wholeness in our nature. When we are in touch with this central core, we experience self-trust and unshakeable faith. Connecting to this core brings us into alignment with what has heart and meaning, and conveys what remains mysterious and transcendent for us all. It is that which makes us unique.

When we are conscious of our character development and spiritual growth, we begin to shift to looking at what is working in our lives and in our own nature. We become happier, healthier, and more effective in our contributions. We begin to look for the goodness in ourselves and others, demonstrating more compassion and generosity.

Obstacles to Gratitude

We would be remiss if we did not touch on the obstacles we may encounter on our gratitude journey. Ralph Waldo Emerson tells us, "Five great enemies to peace inhabit us: avarice, ambition, envy, anger and pride. If those enemies were to be banished, we should infallibly enjoy perpetual peace." Modern life itself, through its many distractions, can erect these barriers to the *practice* of gratitude; these barriers, however, can be overcome by establishing and committing to a gratitude practice, by incorporating the awareness of gratitude into our daily lives. Obstacles to the *experience* of gratitude itself are another matter, and we must be aware of them as we begin this work.

The chief assailants of gratitude are envy, greed, pride, and narcissism. Envy comes from the Latin word *invidia* (looking with malice or coveting what someone else has). Envy and jealousy are qualities that are fed by comparison. The more we compare ourselves to others, or desire what they have, the less satisfied we become with what we currently have; envy creates the perception of lack. As a result, envy also feeds greed—the temptation to hoard as a means of overcompensating for our perceived lack.

Envy and greed are upheld by the hubris and arrogance of pride, which Evagrius Ponticus described as "a tumor of the soul, when it ripens and ruptures, it creates a disgusting mess." In many spiritual traditions it is thought that pride is the worst sin of all because it contains the seed of all other sins. This unhealthy form of pride contains an overpowering need for self-importance and vanity that holds oneself above all else—the law, any person, any faith. Pride, in turn, feeds the state of narcissism, the self-absorption of unsolved ambition and repressed anger that breeds a sense of entitlement and specialness.

All of these states serve as incubators for *ingratitude*. It is important to be aware of them and acknowledge them when they arise, but we need not fear that they carry the power to sabotage our gratitude practice. We each have the ability to shift our awareness to one of "grateful seeing"—noticing first what is working in our lives before dwelling on what we lack or desire but have not yet attained, or on our challenges or burdens. When we look first to the blessings, learnings, mercies, and protections that remain ever present in our lives no matter what our difficulties, it becomes increasingly difficult to sustain a state of ingratitude. Thoreau reminds us that "goodness is the only investment that never fails." Gratitude, the parent of all virtues, is the most fertile ground for growing in virtue. It is our intention of leading a good life, combined with the generation of new perspectives and thoughts, that eradicates the excesses or temptations of avarice, greed, envy, and anger.

Martin Seligman, who has established the field of positive psychology, emphasizes that when we can approach life from the perspective of seeing what is working, without denying our current challenges or burdens, we can cultivate more positive thinking and thankfulness in our lives. Positive and realistic thoughts about what is working in our lives remind us of how blessed we really are.

Gratitude awakens another way of being in the world, one that nurtures the heart and helps to create a life of meaning and purpose. The old barriers no longer confine us and the old fears no longer constrict or claim us. Gratitude opens us to freedom, a sense of generosity, and connection to the wider world.

How to Use This Book to Cultivate a Gratitude-Practice

Living in Gratitude is designed to carry you through a full calendar year, month by month. It approaches the topic of gratitude from a cross-cultural perspective, offering varied tools, maps, and practices based on perennial wisdoms that human beings have explored for centuries. This book is written to be a dependable resource guide and touchstone to gratitude—available to you at any time, no matter what may be happening in your life at the present moment. By creating the opportunity for repeated and sustained gratitude practice, it will help you establish a solid foundation as you shift and begin to embody the true essence of gratitude.

There are many ways to approach using this book—as an individual working alone, with a partner, or in a group. Because the perennial wisdoms are timeless, one can begin this book at any time, or wait until the beginning of the year. Regardless of when the material is approached, it is intention and commitment that will move each individual forward on his or her journey toward a grateful life.

Introduction

Gratitude, Month by Month

Each monthly chapter presents a theme that explores universal, cross-cultural, and perennial wisdoms related to the cultivation of gratitude. The book starts in January with a chapter called *Begin Anew*, offering the opportunity to reopen to life with fresh eyes as a new year commences. February's title is *Attend to the Heart;* here we explore the relationship between gratitude and love. The title for March's chapter is *Compassionate Service,* and in it we consider how gratitude naturally flows from serving others.

April's chapter is called *Mercy and Atonement,* inspired by the many traditions of purification, redemption, and liberation that are associated with this month. In May, we consider *The Gift of Grace,* a state that invites spontaneous gratitude. In June we explore *The Power of Equanimity* as we find ourselves balanced at the midpoint of the year.

July's chapter is *Embracing Nature,* as nature can always inspire gratitude. August invites us toward *Cultivating Peace,* for peacemaking requires us to activate all four portals to gratitude. In September, *Opening to Guidance and Wisdom,* we embrace new pathways to a better life, and with each improvement we make, we renew our experience of gratitude.

The theme of October's chapter is *Letting Be and Letting Go,* and this month offers a time to appreciate things as they are. In November, Thanksgiving month, we practice *Grateful Seeing,* a key concept we have already begun to explore in this introduction. Finally, in December, we investigate the

Mystic Heart, which illuminates winter's darkness and brings spontaneity and joy into our lives.

Reflections and Practices

After the main text for each month, you will find suggested Reflections and Practices. These are designed to foster increased understanding of how the chapter's concepts are at work in your life and to inspire you to cultivate gratitude through action.

Reflection is one of numerous contemplative wisdom practices found in all world traditions. In reflecting, we review, question, and reassess, gaining new insights that may provide us with choices we have not considered before. We learn from and integrate our experience. The questions we are invited to answer in the Reflections section are meant to lead us toward a deeper and more frequent experience of gratitude.

The Practice section is a very important element of each chapter. Whenever we want to learn something new or want change to occur, we must consciously and consistently engage in a practice. Just as we learned to walk, write, and speak through practice, we can change ourselves at any time through its transformative power. Practice develops and transforms us, encourages discipline, and enables us to focus, facilitating change and increased awareness.

Practice is meant to be active, rigorous, and dynamic. While it builds upon reflection and allows us to see what works and what does not, it is not merely reflective, nor is it an exercise in intellectual understanding. To practice is to take daily action that supports change and provides a discipline for incorporating and strengthening new values, skills, and character qualities.

Review and Integration

At the end of every chapter, following the Reflections and Practices sections, which focus on the themes of the month, there are two important and consistent practice sections for review and integration; they are the same for each month. The first practice section, Gratitude in the Four Quadrants of Life, encourages us to look at how gratitude surfaces in each of the four quadrants of work, relationships, finances, and health— as well as in the areas of character development and spiritual growth. The last practice section in every chapter is called Blessings, Learnings, Mercies, and Protections, in which we review and integrate these four portals to gratitude by examining both our current internal and external experiences.

As we explore the exercises contained in this book, gratitude is always our touchstone, active at the center of both contemplation and action. The time and energy we devote to this work bears the richest of fruits: a grateful life.

❦

The human spirit is always reaching for the reclamation of its own well-being. The practice of gratitude provides healing and enhances our inherent nature. The journey that lies before us holds unlimited possibilities filled with blessings, learnings, mercies, and protections awaiting our discovery.

May this journey be marked by unexpected gifts and insights, and an ever expanding awareness of and renewed connection to the very best in ourselves, in others, and in life itself.

{ January }

January Prayer

May We Appreciate and Remember

Today may we appreciate this food

and remember those who are hungry.

May we appreciate our family and friends

and remember those who are alone.

May we appreciate our health

and remember those who are sick.

May we appreciate the freedoms we have

*and remember those who suffer
injustice and tyranny.*

Peace on Earth.

A BUDDHIST BLESSING FOR FOOD

Begin Anew

For all that has been — Thanks!
For all that shall be — Yes!

Dag Hammarskjold

JANUARY IS THE month of new resolve and new beginnings. It is named for the Roman god Janus, the two-headed god whose one head faces the past while the other faces the present and future. As we begin this new year of living in gratitude, we can gaze in both directions. The face that looks back sees a retrospective on what was positive, as well as what was challenging; the face that looks ahead is ever hopeful.

Poet Robinson Jeffers honored this human ability to look both backward and forward when he wrote, "Lend me the stone strength of the past and I will lend you / The wings of the future, for I have them." What do you appreciate today that has roots in the past? What solid, wise, and genuine experiences of your past are calling to be brought forward into your life in the present and future? What winged dreams, hopes, and inspirations do you long to manifest?

This is a good time to appreciate the strengths we have acquired in the past, for these will serve us as we move through the next twelve months. Perhaps we have developed a greater capacity for compassion, or a stronger sense of self-trust. We may find that we have gained courage as a result of our life experience, that we are more solid and secure than in years past. We may have attained a new level of skill in our work, or integrated more healthful choices into our daily life. All such qualities and achievements will enable us to harness the energy of new beginnings and carry it forward throughout the year.

This is also a good time to give thanks for the limitless and exciting possibilities that now lie before us. January offers the opportunity to make a fresh start and do things differently, to go for something we truly want, and to free ourselves from habitual patterns and improve our life at every level: internally and externally; body, mind, and spirit; thought, word, and deed. The traditional season of gift-giving may be behind us, but the gifts that lie before us are plentiful and offer new possibilities for exploration.

Envisioning the Year

At the start of the new year we can begin again to address what Reverend Alan Jones at Grace Cathedral in San Francisco calls the four concerns of life: love, death, power, and time. Each can be seen in the light of new beginnings and of *soulmaking*—daily attention to those things that have heart and meaning for us, and the courage to follow where they lead. Love speaks to our desire for union; death raises questions about our destiny and letting go; power challenges us with issues of vulnerability; and time forces us to see our lives in terms of a play, a drama, or a story. Each year, we encounter all four concerns in our process of unfoldment.

Love, death, power, and time are all universal forces. As the year begins, they challenge each of us to redream and reimagine what is most important for us to bring fully to our attention—and to our intention. In the new year, the love in our heart calls to be deepened, and to release that which no longer serves us. Our renewed power has an opportunity to open to our vulnerabilities and possibilities. Our relationship to time challenges us to trust and reprioritize what is most important for us to address or accomplish during the day. Each year we begin anew to align with these four forces in more imaginative and creative ways. What new relationship do you want to develop with the universal forces of love, death, power, and time this year?

David Cooperrider asserts, "*the creation of positive images on a collective basis . . . might well be the most prolific activity* that individuals and organizations can engage in if their aim is to help bring to fruition a positive and humanly significant future." Images and symbols reveal what currently has meaning for us and what wants our attention. They simultaneously conceal and disclose new possibilities and are often signs or sneak previews of what is emerging for us. As the year commences, what positive images do you hold for yourself, your relationships, your work, and your health? What new possibilities are available to you this year? Now, expand your vision: what do you imagine for your community, your nation, and the world?

Hopi Elder Thomas Banyacya reminds us that in visioning it is important to stop, consider, change, and correct. First we stop, or pause, so we can truly see what is being revealed, or what wants our attention and thoughtful consideration. After we have stopped and considered what we have seen, we can change or take action. As we change and circumstances change, it is important to correct what does not support the vision and its manifestation.

What do you need to stop, consider, change, and correct to better support what you envision for yourself in this new year? For example, you might be drawn to receiving extra training to become more skilled in an art form. Look for and find a workshop that intrigues you. Before you sign up, *stop* to examine the course offering in detail and measure it against your vision. *Consider* its likely impact on your progress—will it truly help you expand your skills to the degree you desire? You may discover that you have set your sights too small, that this short workshop might get you only partway to where you want to go. Now it's time to revisit your vision and *change* it—widen and broaden it. To expand your possibilities, you may need to course-*correct.* Perhaps something more intensive is in order, such as finding a highly skilled mentor or engaging in a longer period of study.

The stop, consider, change, and correct practice offers a way to align our vision with our choices. Banyaca offers a powerful way to direct our own future, to manifest what we truly want in our life. Contained within the practice is the ever present opportunity to begin anew. This practice is of special value in January as we contemplate the opportunities that now lie before us, but it can serve us at any time. In working with it this month, we have a new tool that will serve us well throughout the year.

Welcoming the Unexpected

As we move through Janus's month—looking behind us and investigating our memories, looking before us and conjuring dreams of the future—it is important to welcome, with gratitude, the unexpected. As psychologist and scholar of archetypal collective imagery C. G. Jung wrote, "there is in the psyche, a process that seeks its own goal, no matter what the external factors may be." This is the soul's persistent way of manifesting what is true for us in the four areas of love, death, power, and time, and it often does so in surprising ways.

When we have not been paying close attention to how we are living, the psyche will step in with unexpected events. We may busily be working on improving a relationship, for example, thinking it is our most urgent task at hand, only to be reminded—perhaps by a sudden unforeseen expense—that what we really need to attend to is our financial solvency. The psyche will send us persistent messages to let us know what our real work is, and often these messages come through surprising events that get our attention and help us realize that our ego's perceived agenda is not aligned with the psyche's agenda or our own integrity. As we begin a new year, it is important to pay attention to repeated events that may run counter to our ego's ideas of where we think we are going, and that point to the actual work that is before us.

Entering the Year with Childlike Curiosity

With January comes the wonderful possibility to reenter the world with fresh eyes, reclaimed innocence, and a blank slate. We have the opportunity to approach this year with childlike curiosity and openness, and to explore the new and the unknown in our lives. As we go forth into the new year, perhaps we can heed the wisdom found in this Sufi story by al-Ghazzali:

> A sheikh said, "If you wish to become a saint, change your character into the character of children."
>
> "Why?" he was asked.
>
> "Children have five qualities," he answered, "and if adults had these same qualities, they would attain the rank of saints."
>
> 1. They do not worry about their daily bread.
>
> 2. When they fall sick, they do not complain night and day about their misfortune.
>
> 3. Whatever food they have, they share.

4. When they fight or quarrel, they do not keep grudges in their hearts, but make up quickly.

5. The slightest threat makes them frightened and brings tears to their eyes."

We may not desire to become saints, but entering the year with the innocence of a child generates fresh perspectives and creative options.

January's celebration of the Epiphany—or Three Kings Day, named for the three magi who followed the star to find the infant Jesus—is a way of honoring the Divine Child and sacred mystery within us all. This is the part of us that is whole, open, curious, vulnerable, clear, and loving. We often use the word epiphany to describe or suggest an experience of illumination or awakening. To say that someone has had an epiphany is to say that he or she has had a profound insight, or has made an illuminating discovery that is significant and meaningful and provides a motivation to change (just as the magi discovered the infant Jesus). At the beginning of each new year, we are always reminded of the opportunity to begin anew with childlike wonder, a state that invites and welcomes epiphanies or "aha moments." These revelations remind us of the mystery of life's journey, which is renewed each year in the month of January.

⁓

January is a time to bring the gifts of the past forward into our present and future. This allows us to continue to build on the wisdom we have gained throughout our life experience. The month brings with it the opportunity to reopen to life and embrace it with renewed enthusiasm, hope, and childlike wonder. An abundance of blessings, learnings, mercies, and protections is in store for us as the year unfolds. Here at the start, let us set the intention to take note of each blessing, learning, mercy, and protection as we find it, to celebrate it well, and to enter frequently and joyfully into the life-changing state of being that is gratitude.

JANUARY BENEFIT OF GRATITUDE-PRACTICE

Robert A. Emmons and Michael E. McCullough are currently the foremost researchers to demonstrate the positive impact gratitude practices have on human beings. Their work is synthesized in their groundbreaking book *The Psychology of Gratitude*. One of their findings reveals that "grateful people tend to be happy people"; and the daily practice of gratitude significantly increases happiness and states of well-being within human beings.

The field of positive psychology and the research of Martin Seligman also verify that positive and optimistic people experience more happiness and tend to be more grateful.

Reflections

The part of us that wants to become is fearless.

JOSEPH CAMPBELL

In contemplative practices of any kind, questions provoke inquiry, reflection, and conscious awareness of what we are learning or what is being revealed to us about our own current inner and outer work.

Notice which of the following questions capture your attention and which are less evocative or interesting to you at this time. Select two or three of the most meaningful questions for you and explore them more deeply.

• Like the mythical god Janus, and as reflected in the Robinson Jeffers quote at the beginning of this chapter, are you gathering "the stone strength of the past" and "the wings of the future"? What circumstances are requiring you to draw upon both?

• What are you learning from the four themes of soulmaking and new beginnings this month?

Love—Your desire for union and meaningful connection.

Death—Your ability to release, let go, and surrender.

Power—Your ability to sustain right use of power and stay connected to your heart and your integrity.

Time—Your relationship to time reveals your capacity to trust that whatever is present each day, you can handle; otherwise it would not be there. The surprising or unexpected happenings of each day reveal your attachments and teach you about your ability or inability to remain flexible.

- In what ways are you manifesting the five simple qualities of childlike openness?

  Not worrying about your daily bread
  Not complaining when you fall sick
  Sharing whatever you have
  When you fight or quarrel, not holding a grudge and making up quickly
  Showing your vulnerability when frightened or threatened

- What epiphanies or new insights are motivating positive changes for you at this time?

- What childlike curiosity and wonder are you currently bringing to your work, relationships, finances, health, and personal growth?

- For the month of January, track those experiences for which you are particularly grateful. How have they contributed to your happiness and well-being?

January: Begin Anew

Practices

Practices are essential for integrating what we are learning. Select two or three of the following practices that most specifically apply to your current experience and would help you the most at this time.

- Create your own gratitude poem, prayer, or saying for this month.

- Start your own meaningful collection of gratitude materials. What family prayers have been passed on to you? What poems or passages of literature have you committed to memory? Remember that anything you have committed to memory has meaning for you.

- Practice the Hopi Elder's advice before beginning anew: stop, consider, change and correct in the quadrants of work, relationships, health, and finances.

- At the end of each day, notice what or who made you happy. Silently give gratitude for each person or circumstance that brought joy into your life on this day.

- Each week, choose to experience something new; do something that you have not done before. New experiences offer new possibilities and opportunities for growth.

- Take an action every day to support and strengthen your right relationship with and connection to the resources of love, death, power, and time.

Review and Integration

Gratitude in the Four Quadrants of Life

work　　　　　　　　*relationships*

**SPIRITUAL GROWTH &
DEVELOPING CHARACTER**

finances　　　　　　　　*health*

Notice what you are grateful for in the four quadrants of your life:

- Work/creative service

- Relationships: friends, colleagues, and family

- Finances and right livelihood

- Health and well-being

The center of the four quadrants represents the place of *developing character* and connecting to your own *spiritual growth* and development. The center is influenced, impacted, and informed by all four quadrants. To help you discover the sources of your gratitude, answer the following tracking questions and see which quadrant or quadrants are emphasized more for you this month.

In looking at the illustration of the Four Quadrants of Life, consider the following questions:

- What are you seeing that is similar to last month's work? What is different, or significantly changing? Review the four quadrants of your life. What is being most activated in either your work, relationships, finances, or health?

- What internal insights and discoveries are you making that have strengthened your character and fostered spiritual growth this month?

- What are you noticing that is new, expanded, or being released in each quadrant of your life this month?

- What are you grateful for in each of your life's quadrants, and how are you expressing your thankfulness?

Blessings, Learnings, Mercies, and Protections

blessings

mercies   protections

learnings

Express your gratitude by reflecting upon:

- The major *Blessings* you have given and received during January.

- The major *Learnings* you have given and received during January.

- The major *Mercies* you have given and received during January.

- The major *Protections* you have given and received during January.

The following questions can help you go deeper in your exploration of these four portals to gratitude.

External Questions

- Who or what has inspired you?

- Who or what is challenging you?

- Who or what is surprising you?

- Who or what is touching or moving you?

Internal Questions

- What is strengthening within my nature?

- What is softening within my nature?

- What is opening within my nature?

- What is deepening within my nature?

{ February }

February Prayer

For Success

Lord, behold our family here assembled.
We thank thee for this place in which we dwell,
for the love that unites us, for the peace
accorded to us this day, for the hope with
which we expect the morrow, for the health,
the work, the food and the bright skies
that make our lives delightful; for our friends
in all parts of the earth. Amen.

FROM ROBERT LOUIS STEVENSON'S
PRAYERS WRITTEN AT VAILIMA

Attend to
the Heart

God gave you a gift of 86,400 seconds today.
Have you used one today to say "thank you"?

WILLIAM A. WARD

FEBRUARY IS THE month when we consciously review what touches our hearts. Valentine's Day is the primary celebration this month. We enjoy it with our families and friends, in schools and in workplaces. It provides us with a community-wide, collective opportunity to reflect upon whom and what we love.

The heart is the central place where we learn about love, and it is in our hearts that we discover what is truly meaningful. What we are learning about love now surfaces for review, as does gratitude for those people and circumstances that are teaching us about love.

Brother David Steindl-Rast has written about the inseparable relationship between the heart, love, and gratefulness in his book *Gratefulness, the Heart of Prayer*. He describes this triune relationship as follows: "The heart is where we belong. We belong there as to our proper place, no matter how estranged we have become. And when we are there we belong, because what makes home home is that each belongs to all and all to each . . ." "We grow in love when we grow in gratefulness. And we grow in gratefulness when we love . . . This makes gratefulness a school in which one learns love."

All spiritual traditions give voice to the truth that love is stronger than fear, hatred, or indifference. Perhaps then, our greatest practice as we move through the last full month of winter is to choose to experience this universal spiritual truth in our own lives—to make a conscious decision to immerse ourselves in the light and warmth of the heart. We can choose, and choose again as the need arises, to redirect our attention away from worries and resentments, shake ourselves loose from apathy and indifference, and focus our awareness—from moment to moment, hour by hour—upon tenderness and affection. We always have the opportunity and choice to express the love that flows between us and within our circles of influence, and extend it to all living peoples, creatures, and plants.

A wonderful example of this is how Myrlie Evers described one way in which her husband, Medgar Evers, the heroic civil rights leader, demonstrated his love and gratitude for her:

I love roses, but Medgar could never afford to buy me a florist's bouquet. So he did something better. Every year he made a ritual of giving me bare-root roses to plant in our yard, and eventually, three dozen rose-bushes were the envy of our neighbors. Once in awhile, Medgar would gather a bouquet, or perhaps just one rose, and hand it to me as he came through the door. It became an unspoken verse of the love between us.

The month of February offers daily opportunities to both say aloud what is in our hearts and communicate our love through our actions: our own "unspoken verses of love."

It is equally important to express the spoken verses of love and the demonstrative actions of love. In her book *The Second Shift*, Arlie Hochschild coined the phrase "economy of gratitude" with respect to marriages and committed relationships. She writes, "When couples struggle, it is seldom over who does what. Far more often, it is over the giving and receiving of gratitude. When gratitude is expressed either in word or action to our loved ones, they experience being cherished and valued rather than taken for granted or disrespected."

To learn how people want to be loved, we need only look at the way *they* love. Take a moment now to consider how you cherish and express your love for others. Recall a time when you spoke loving words to another or showed your love through a generous act. Remember what you said or did and the circumstances that prompted your expression of love. Through your recollections, you have just described to yourself some of the ways you would like to be loved.

The Four-Chambered Heart

The practice of gratitude keeps our hearts open: it is impossible to extend gratitude when our hearts are closed. With an open heart, we can access and bring forth the love that is in our nature waiting to be expressed. In order to know what is in our hearts, it is important to attend to the four-chambered heart: the *full, strong, open, and clear* heart. Each chamber is an invitation to live in gratitude.

Where we are *full-hearted* in our lives, we are deeply engaged, responsible, reliable, and committed. The *strong heart* demonstrates courage; it neither avoids conflict nor seeks approval from others. The *open heart* releases attachments and opens us to compassion and mercy, which draw forth the power of genuine apology and forgiveness work. The *clear heart* expresses wisdom. Nothing creates more safety in our relationships than the expression of clarity.

Examples of full-hearted people are Eleanor Roosevelt and Martin Luther King Jr. Both were committed to human rights and were passionate about creating change. Roosevelt was the driving force behind the United Nations' Universal Declaration of Human Rights. King established the civil rights movement. The passion of a full-hearted life can express itself in many other ways as well. To recognize your own full-heartedness, notice where you are fully engaged in manifesting what has heart and meaning for you, whether it is in painting, writing, gardening, creating, or leading others.

We are strong-hearted whenever we demonstrate courage in our lives, such as by standing up for a friend who is being treated unjustly, or by intervening when someone is being bullied. Courage means standing by one's heart or core. When we are courageous we are able to meet conflict without fear. In what situation have you recently demonstrated courage or strong-heartedness in your life? Recognize your strength of heart as something for which to be grateful.

Openheartedness is apparent in people whose curiosity is greater than their criticality. Children are natural explorers and discoverers because their curiosity and commitment to learning are greater than their self-consciousness or defensiveness. Openhearted people demonstrate more compassion, kindness, and generosity as a result of the delight they take in maintaining their sense of adventure and wonder. We encounter our own openheartedness when we can set aside our preconceived notions and simply ask, "What is here to be discovered?"

Clarity of heart creates safety in all relationships and circumstances, and there are always points of clarity to explore. When our hearts are clear, we know where we stand with the important people in our lives. For example, in a relationship, we may be clear that we both feel great affection for one another, but not so clear about what form the relationship should take or what level of commitment exists. In a work setting, we may be clear that we are highly skilled in two areas of specialty, and also know that we have enormous contributions to make in other areas. However, we may not yet be clear about whether we want to take on any additional projects at this time. In both of these examples, we may be tempted to take premature action, such as impulsively committing to a relationship or signing up for a heavier workload, and we may later come to regret our actions. A clear heart, in contrast, galvanizes appropriate action.

Toward a Healthy Four-Chambered Heart

When the four-chambered heart is full, strong, open, and clear, it is healthy, and gratitude comes to us naturally. We choose to live a meaningful life filled with integrity and purpose, one that offers unlimited ways to be thankful and to express our gratitude to those around us. However, it is not always easy to abide in these states consistently, and some of them may be more challenging than others for us to realize and to integrate. At times we might lapse into their opposites, becoming half-hearted, weak-hearted, closed-hearted, or confused-hearted. Although these states are a part of human nature, a healthy heart weans itself from these distorted and unhealthy ways. The first step to doing this is to recognize these states when they surface.

When we are half-hearted, we operate from "shoulds" rather than wants. Often, half-heartedness signals when we feel duty-bound and believe we have little or no choice in what we do. We are not consistent or reliable when we are half-hearted. Half-heartedness can also indicate that we have outgrown certain interests, people, or circumstances.

Weak-heartedness is present whenever we have difficulty facing conflict or are in great need of acceptance and approval from others. We often move into denial when we are weak-hearted so we won't have to see things as they are. We may choose to ignore potential signs of an affair, for example, rationalizing that our spouse's sudden closeness with a coworker can only be work related. Discovering the truth would lead to conflict, and in our weak-hearted state, we prefer to deceive ourselves. Or we may witness a family member's act of violence—throwing a plate against the wall, for instance—and rather than confront the behavior, we tell ourselves that everyone needs to let off steam once in a while. When we are weak-hearted and in denial, we normalize the abnormal and abnormalize the normal.

Any closed-heartedness in our nature shows us where we are still holding on to old resentments, grudges, or disappointments, and reveals to us where we have forgiveness work to do. When our hearts are closed we can be punitive, withholding, blaming, and critical of ourselves and others. What do you recognize or observe about your own closed-heartedness at this time? What do you need to forgive now in yourself and others?

Confused-heartedness shows us where we lack clarity, and in this state we may profess confusion. However, our confusion may actually be a manufactured camouflage for our unwillingness to be clear. We might tell a lover, for example, that we're confused about where our relationship is going rather than state what we are clear about and what we are not. In this way, we place the responsibility for a decision about the relationship on the other person—combining confused-heartedness with weak-heartedness. Doubt, confusion, ambivalence, and hesitation are conditions that create a lack of safety in any relationship.

Any or all of these states may sound familiar to you; they are human tendencies. In gratitude work, we notice them when they arise, and we make a conscious decision to shift our heart's stance to one of fullness, strength, openness, and clarity. Each victory in this direction becomes its own source of gratitude as we grow spiritually and deepen our character.

A Gratitude-Building Exercise from the Dalai Lama

The Dalai Lama offers a practice that cultivates love and happiness in our nature and supports the expression of love and compassion in all situations. This practice also supports the four-chambered heart in remaining full, strong, open, and clear in its expression, which in turn allows us to fully engage in appreciation and thankfulness.

1. Spend five minutes at the beginning of each day remembering that we all want the same thing: to be happy, to be loved, and to feel connected.

2. Spend five minutes cherishing yourself and others. Let go of judgments. Breathe in cherishing yourself, and

breathe out cherishing others. If the faces of people you are having trouble with appear, cherish them as well.

3. During the day, extend that attitude to everyone you meet—we are all the same—with "I cherish myself and you too (the store clerk, the client, a family member, a coworker, a fellow bus-rider)."

4. Stay in the practice no matter what happens! (Disarmingly simple, though not necessarily easy.)

Robert Emmons's research supports the Dalai Lama's practice of extending compassion to ourselves and others. Emmons says, "Encouraging people to focus on the benefits they have received from others leads them to feel loved and cared for by others. So gratitude appears to build friendships and other social bonds."

❧

February affords us the time to reflect upon and attend to our heart work. As Brother David Steindl-Rast shows us, when we are at home in our hearts, love and gratefulness always increase. The Dalai Lama's practice allows us to cultivate interdependence by consciously extending empathy and respect to each other through cherishing ourselves and others as we breathe. When we combine this practice with clearing the four-chambered heart to restore its natural state of whole-heartedness, we foster increased love, and this allows gratitude to become more abundant in our lives.

FEBRUARY BENEFIT OF GRATITUDE-PRACTICE

❦

Did you know that couples who express more gratitude and appreciation for each other rather than complaints stay together longer? John Gottman's two decades of research at the University of Washington on marital relations reveals that couples who express at least a five-to-one ratio of appreciations to complaints stay married and increase their longevity together. Those who have more complaints than appreciation are more apt to divorce or separate. Practice increasing your own five-to-one ratio in all your relations this month.

Reflections

What the world really needs is more love and less paperwork.

PEARL BAILEY

In contemplative practices of any kind, questions provoke inquiry, reflection, and conscious awareness of what we are learning or what is being revealed to us about our own current inner and outer work.

Notice which of the following questions capture your attention and which are less evocative or interesting to you at this time. Select two or three of the most meaningful questions for you and explore them more deeply.

- Who have been the teachers of your heart in the past? What are you currently learning about love? Who are your current teachers of the heart?

- Attend daily to the four-chambered heart:

  In what areas of your life do you feel half-hearted rather than full-hearted?

  Where do you feel weak-hearted rather than strong-hearted?

  Where are you closed-hearted when you could be open-hearted?

  In what ways are you confused or doubting rather than clear-hearted?

- Review the Dalai Lama's four practices: Which ones are consistently easy for you to sustain on a daily basis? Which are challenging?

- What are you currently learning about love? How are the people around you manifesting love? This can tell you how they themselves want to be loved.

- In what specific ways are you being more expressive and demonstrative in your love and gratefulness?

Practices

Practices are essential for integrating what we are learning. Select two or three of the following practices that most specifically apply to your current experience and would help you the most at this time.

- Each day this month, take an action that brings more love into the world and relieves suffering: acts of service, communicating gratitude, acknowledging others' presence and gifts, acting in kindness, or expressing joy. What are your strongest experiences?

- Practice making a conscious choice to shift your attention from worries and resentments and place it upon tenderness and affection. What do you observe?

- At the beginning of each week, create a plan for expressing love in the four quadrants of your life: work, relationships, health, and generating abundance. Write down one action you plan to take to express love in each quadrant. Post this list in a place where you will see it so that you do not forget to put your plan into action.

- Write down an obstacle that seems to get in the way of your expressing love or gratitude. Then imagine the antidote to this obstacle and write this down as well. For example, one obstacle may be something you and your friend, coworker, or family member have not done very often before. If that is the case, you might write:

Obstacle: We don't usually openly express these feelings with each other, so we might feel uncomfortable. **Antidote:** Over time, we can transform something unusual into something that is welcome and comes naturally and easily. I will accept some discomfort (be strong-hearted) for now and take the first step. Then tomorrow, I'll take the next . . .

- Choose in advance a particular day this month to notice the many ways people express affection and love. On that day, carrying a small notebook with you, set out to observe any expressions of love that may occur around you. Notice a kind word, a gentle pat, a protective gesture, a bright beaming smile, a shared good-hearted laugh. Write these down as they happen, or as soon as you can. Choose the ones that most deeply moved you, then notice when *you* express your love in these similar or different ways.

Review and Integration

Gratitude in the Four Quadrants of Life

work *relationships*

**SPIRITUAL GROWTH &
DEVELOPING CHARACTER**

finances *health*

Notice what you are grateful for in the four quadrants of your life:

- Work/creative service

- Relationships: friends, colleagues, and family

- Finances and right livelihood

- Health and well-being

February: Attend to the Heart

The center of the four quadrants represents the place of *developing character* and connecting to your own *spiritual growth* and development. The center is influenced, impacted, and informed by all four quadrants. To help you discover the sources of your gratitude, answer the following tracking questions and see which quadrant or quadrants are emphasized more for you this month.

In looking at the illustration of the Four Quadrants of Life, consider the following questions:

- What are you seeing that is similar to last month's work? What is different, or significantly changing? Review the four quadrants of your life. What is being most activated in either your work, relationships, finances, or health?

- What internal insights and discoveries are you making that have strengthened your character and fostered spiritual growth this month?

- What are you noticing that is new, expanded, or being released in each quadrant of your life this month?

- What are you grateful for in each of your life's quadrants, and how are you expressing your thankfulness?

Blessings, Learnings, Mercies, and Protections

Express your gratitude by reflecting upon:

- The major *Blessings* you have given and received during February.

- The major *Learnings* you have given and received during February.

- The major *Mercies* you have given and received during February.

- The major *Protections* you have given and received during February.

The following questions can help you go deeper in your exploration of these four portals to gratitude.

External Questions

- Who or what has inspired you?

- Who or what is challenging you?

- Who or what is surprising you?

- Who or what is touching or moving you?

Internal Questions

- What is strengthening within my nature?

- What is softening within my nature?

- What is opening within my nature?

- What is deepening within my nature?

{ March }

March Prayer

Recall the face

*of the poorest and the weakest man
whom you may have seen,*

*and ask yourself, if the step you contemplate
is going to be of any use to him . . . .*

*Will it restore him to a control over
his own life and destiny?*

*Will it lead to self-rule for the hungry
and spiritually starving millions?*

*Then you will find your doubts
and your self melt away.*

MOHANDAS GANDHI (1869–1948)

Compassionate Service

To be grateful is to recognize the Love of God
in everything He has given us.

THOMAS MERTON

MARCH STANDS AT the cusp of winter and spring. With the arrival of the vernal equinox around the twenty-first of the month, we enter the season when fresh new life bursts into being with exuberance and vigor. In calendars preceding our current one, the new year began in March, because that was when winter's starkness gave way to tiny buds, emerging green leaves, blossoming trees, and opening flowers.

Hildegard von Bingen referred to this time as *veriditas,* the true greening of ourselves and nature. Those things that have been gestating and incubating in winter reveal themselves in spring, and it is during this bourgeoning time that nature mirrors back to us new possibilities and the exaltation of life. The poet George Herbert, after experiencing a period of depression, or spiritual wasteland, wrote, "Who would have thought my shrivel'd heart could have recovered greenness?"

Spring is the season of hope and the irresistible impulse to grow and create. As we notice vibrant green shoots pushing up out of the earth and hear songbirds call for their mates, our own natures begin to realign with the inherent beauty, goodness, and abundance that surround us. These qualities always reside in the human spirit; if they have been dormant during winter, or beyond the range of our attention, they are brought to life and into focus by nature's spring splendor.

Ways to Become a Better Person: Compassionate Service

The Irish St. Patrick's Day celebration in March reminds us that we have the opportunity to empower ourselves, to regrow and "regreen" ourselves. The Irish shamrocks and leprechauns that are part of this annual ritual are metaphors for hope and magical possibilities. We are reminded at this time of year that "luck" is actually where opportunities and preparedness intersect.

We have the ultimate opportunity in spring to restore and embody our natural goodness, to harness our luck, and to become better people. As Abraham Maslow reminds us in *Religions, Values, and Peak Experiences,* "the best way to become a better 'helper' is to become a better person. But one necessary aspect of becoming a better person is *via* helping other people. So one must and can do both simultaneously." This is a good time to think about the areas of your life where you want to become a better person in order to help others in more impactful ways.

One of the best set of practices for becoming a better person through cultivating compassionate service comes from Ram Dass and Mirabai Bush in their book *Compassion in Action: Setting Out on a Path of Service*. In this book, we are advised to:

- be brave

- start small

- use what you've got

- do something you enjoy

- don't overcommit

We must be discerning when we move forward with any new intention—being attentive to that which is before us and seeking insights into its meaning. Discernment carries the same requirements as Dass and Bush's five tenets. We need to summon the courage to begin a new phase in our growth; then we can start with something we are confident we can achieve. By taking one deliberate step each day, we avoid recklessness and can build upon those beneficial traits we have already developed in ourselves. Once we align with our hearts to do what we enjoy, then we can choose not to struggle, push, or overcommit. In this way we can find and experience harmony between our souls and the way we are living our lives.

One way to understand the lessons of the five tenets is to draw upon memories of learning. Remember when you first learned how to ride a bike or to ski. You wanted to learn because you thought it would be exhilarating and fun; you began with the anticipation of enjoyment. From there, the rest of the tenets fell into place: you started small, perhaps with training wheels and an adult trotting along beside you, or on the easiest ski slope under the watchful eye of a family member, friend, or instructor. You summoned the courage to fling yourself into the unknown, using only what you had— your enthusiasm and whatever level of strength and balance you had already achieved. And, most likely, you stopped when you became tired, choosing to come back to the bike or the skis another day and improve your skills over time.

When we make the choice to become a better person, these same dynamics come into play. Whether we are volunteering for the first time or starting an entirely new enterprise to help others, we are applying the same essential principles that enabled us to move from a tentative start in the driveway to confidently taking the bike path to school or to play.

Author Karen Armstrong found a unique way to contribute to the human family and the planet by working to bring compassion back into the heart of society. Her adventure started with the tenet of using what she had.

When she received a large cash prize from an organization, accompanied by the charge that she must use it to grant a wish for a better world, she felt no hesitation about what she would do. In 2009, she established the international Charter for Compassion. Tens of thousands of people of all walks of life, nationalities, beliefs, and backgrounds contributed to the first draft of the charter, the intent of which was to unify, inspire, and increase awareness of compassion as an active expression of reciprocity and mutuality. From this abundance of contributions, the charter was revised into a succinct statement, and today people around the world are at work transforming it into action. This is but one example of what can be accomplished when we choose to engage in generous acts. A worldwide movement began with one person's abiding passion coupled with an unexpected opportunity.

Preceding this effort, in 1956, Global Impact was one of the very first nonprofit organizations dedicated to helping the world's most vulnerable people. It is the national leader in raising awareness and funds for humanitarian organizations and provides quality programs for disaster relief, education, health care training, and economic solvency. Global Impact continues to model various forms of compassionate service worldwide by promoting hope, self-sufficiency, and help to people and communities in need.

Compassionate generosity and gratitude are inextricably linked. Sociologist Georg Simmel (1858–1918) wrote one of the earliest essays addressing the subject of gratitude, entitled "Faithfulness and gratitude." He called gratitude "the moral memory of mankind," asserting that "by mutual giving, people become tied to each other by a web of feelings of gratitude. Gratitude is the motive that moves us to give in return and thus creates the reciprocity of service and counterservice." At the times when you feel most grateful, where do you find shared mutuality and reciprocity in your life? By striving to become a better person through giving your time, talents, and resources to others, you reap the rewards of appreciation and thankfulness. The experience of reciprocity establishes a heartfelt connection and recognition of what provides the foundation for compassionate service in our lives.

❧

Because March moves us from barren winter to verdant spring, the experience of gratitude now wells up within us more easily and often. In Brian Boyd's *Vladimir Nabokov: The American Years,* Nabokov beautifully describes this experience: "This is ecstasy, and behind the ecstasy is something else, which is hard to explain. It is like a momentary vacuum into which rushes all that I love. A sense of oneness with sun and stone. A thrill of gratitude." Notice during this month of March what ignites the "thrill of gratitude" in your life. When we couple this natural upwelling with conscious acts of compassionate service, our experience of gratitude is magnified a hundredfold. During this season of veriditas, we experience the greening of ourselves and the natural world.

MARCH BENEFIT OF GRATITUDE-PRACTICE

Did you know that the practice of gratitude increases compassion, reciprocity, and mutuality? Sociologist Georg Simmel conducted a mental experiment by imagining what would happen if every grateful action based on benefits received in the past were suddenly eliminated. He determined that society would fall apart. "Gratitude not only creates and smoothens interpersonal relationships; it also fulfills important cohesive functions for society and culture as such." Compassionate service cultivates mutuality, reciprocity, and gratitude. Where are you involved in compassionate service in your life at this time?

Reflections

Embody the love, gratitude, and compassion you want
to promote.

DENNIS RIVERS

In contemplative practices of any kind, questions provoke inquiry, reflection, and conscious awareness of what we are learning or what is being revealed to us about our own current inner and outer work.

Notice which of the following questions capture your attention and which are less evocative or interesting to you at this time. Select two or three of the most meaningful questions for you and explore them more deeply.

- Take time each day to pause and reflect upon Hildegard von Bingen's concept of veriditas—that spring invites us toward the true greening of ourselves and nature. What is newly green and growing in your nature at this time?

- What have you been incubating or gestating in winter that is now emerging in spring? What new possibilities are opening for you?

- Where is *luck* present in your life? Remember, luck is actually where opportunity and preparedness intersect. If something lucky has come along, consider how you have set the stage to welcome it, and explore the opportunities it contains.

- The practice of gratitude keeps the heart open; discernment is wisdom's way to ensure we take appropriate and wise action to connect with what has heart and meaning for us. What wise actions of thankfulness and generosity do you want to extend to yourself and others this month?

- Notice this month where you have extended compassion to others. Where have others extended compassion to you?

- What is igniting the "thrill of gratitude" in your life this month? Offer thanks and appreciation for those moments that Nabokov describes as "a momentary vacuum into which rushes all that I love." What does such a moment feel like in your body? What emotions arise?

Practices

Practices are essential for integrating what we are learning. Select two or three of the following practices that most specifically apply to your current experience and would help you the most at this time.

- Read this chapter's opening invocation by Gandhi every day and notice what impact it has on your compassionate service or what changes you make as a result of reading this every day this month.

- Take time every day to rest and renew yourself. This is an active intention for *regreening your nature and releasing any stress*. This practice reinforces poet George Herbert's insight, "Who would have thought my shrivel'd heart could have recovered greenness?"

- Practice Ram Dass and Mirabai Bush's five ways of cultivating compassionate service; and, as a result, become what Maslow calls, "a better person":

  be brave
  start small
  use what you've got
  do something you enjoy
  don't overcommit
  Note which of these may come most naturally to you and which are more challenging.

- Perform a compassionate act every day this month.

- Hold a monthly gratitude circle for friends, colleagues, family, or others with whom you are called to share this practice. Notice where your experiences are similar and where they are different or unique. How does sharing your practice with others change your experience?

- Offer gratitude to yourself for who you are and who you are becoming. Write down five things that you are most grateful for that have changed within your own nature this month.

Review and Integration

Gratitude in the Four Quadrants of Life

work *relationships*

**SPIRITUAL GROWTH &
DEVELOPING CHARACTER**

finances *health*

Notice what you are grateful for in the four quadrants of your life:

- Work/creative service

- Relationships: friends, colleagues, and family

- Finances and right livelihood

- Health and well-being

The center of the four quadrants represents the place of *developing character* and connecting to your own *spiritual growth* and development. The center is influenced, impacted, and informed by all four quadrants. To help you discover the sources of your gratitude, answer the following tracking questions and see which quadrant or quadrants are emphasized more for you this month.

In looking at the illustration of the Four Quadrants of Life, consider the following questions:

- What are you seeing that is similar to last month's work? What is different, or significantly changing? Review the four quadrants of your life. What is being most activated in either your work, relationships, finances, or health?

- What internal insights and discoveries are you making that have strengthened your character and fostered spiritual growth this month?

- What are you noticing that is new, expanded, or being released in each quadrant of your life this month?

- What are you grateful for in each of your life's quadrants, and how are you expressing your thankfulness?

March: Compassionate Service

Blessings, Learnings, Mercies, and Protections

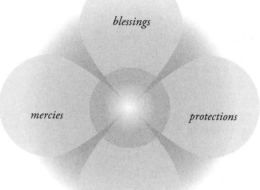

Express your gratitude by reflecting upon:

- The major *Blessings* you have given and received during March.

- The major *Learnings* you have given and received during March.

- The major *Mercies* you have given and received during March.

- The major *Protections* you have given and received during March.

The following questions can help you go deeper in your exploration of these four portals to gratitude.

External Questions

- Who or what has inspired you?

- Who or what is challenging you?

- Who or what is surprising you?

- Who or what is touching or moving you?

Internal Questions

- What is strengthening within my nature?

- What is softening within my nature?

- What is opening within my nature?

- What is deepening within my nature?

{ April }

April Prayer

Oh, give us pleasure in the flowers to-day;
And give us not to think so far away
As the uncertain harvest; keep us here
All simply in the springing of the year.

Oh, give us pleasure in the orchard white,
Like nothing else by day, like ghosts by night;
And make us happy in the happy bees,
The swarm dilating round the perfect trees.

And make us happy in the darting bird,
That suddenly above the bees is heard,
The meteor that thrusts with needle bill,
And off a blossom in midair stands still.

For this is love and nothing else is love,
That which is reserved for God above
To sanctify to what far ends He will,
But which it only needs that we fulfill.

ROBERT FROST, FROM *A BOY'S WILL*

Mercy and Atonement

Gratitude is the fairest blossom
which springs from the souls.

HENRY WARD BEECHER

APRIL USHERS IN the exuberance of spring. The month begins with April Fools' Day, the day of the trickster, when we test our gullibility in a playful, good-natured way, without doing harm. When we discover we have been fooled and feel a little chagrined, we cannot help but laugh, as we take a secret delight in our own naiveté. This sets the tone for spring's joyous purpose, which Frost describes so well: "to make us happy in the happy bees . . . And make us happy in the darting bird." Ultimately, spring's way is to compel us to enjoy all that is fresh, new, and unexpected, and to rejoice in the emergence of life.

It is a challenge to be unhappy during this season of vibrant growth, and it is easy to experience spontaneous outpourings of gratitude. With the lengthening daylight, the vivid colors of blossoming trees, and the subtle scent of warming earth, our sensory experiences call to us again and again, reminding us of the miracles found at every turn. We can be startled into thankfulness at any moment during this time of year.

April's Spiritual Meanings

April has great significance in the many spiritual traditions of the world. Depending upon the tradition in question, it can be a time of sanctification, purification, surrender, redemption, liberation, or resurrection. The word *Islam* itself means surrender: to submit one's life to God. The daily Islamic practices of prayer and bowing are acts of surrender and extending honor to God's will. In the Judaic tradition, Passover offers an opportunity to be liberated from selfishness, to grow in love, and ultimately to become love. Easter is the time when Christians celebrate the purification inherent in redemption, liberation, and resurrection. In his book *The Redemptive Self: Stories Americans Live By*, D. P. McAdams has found that personal redemption and expressions of deep gratitude are consistent themes in the lives of highly generative people: those who produce benefit for themselves and others. "Among the most generative adults, the desire to express gratitude for the benefits enjoyed in life, or even for life itself, become something of a credo in their life stories." In all the spiritual traditions and redemption stories, human beings return to and experience the natural states of freedom, love, humility, and goodness. So it is that April holds the twin blessings of nature's spectacular renewal and the soul's sanctification and redemption.

The Release of Ingratitude

In April, the liberating powers of mercy and forgiveness are present, and we have the opportunity to release corrosive states of ingratitude. We can use this time to free ourselves from pride, narcissism, or a sense of entitlement; to turn away from comparisons with others and envy of what they may have; and to release our stored anger, resentment, hatred, and disappointment. We can drop our illusions and meet life honestly, just as it is. During this month, our gratitude work is to expose the states of ungratefulness we harbor within ourselves. We may have long practiced turning from them—reluctant to recognize such qualities within ourselves—but now they are calling for healing so we may restore balance to our relationships, with others and ourselves.

The philosopher Immanuel Kant recognized that ingratitude is the refusal to acknowledge the good, and as a result is a profound moral failure of the human spirit. He strongly named the state of ingratitude as a character flaw in this much repeated quote: "Ingratitude is the essence of vileness."

The moral code of reciprocity—give and take, which is intrinsic to human beings, holds that reciprocity is violated when we are not grateful for what we have received, especially if we *habitually respond* from indifference, jealousy, pride, or resentment. Universally, this is a flagrant violation of natural law, which Kant recognized very early in his career. When we begin to take our blessings for granted, or constantly compare ourselves to and become envious of others, we are in states of ingratitude. Often, being ungrateful can be a symptom of mistrust, suspicion of another's motives, or lack of socialization. It can also be a way to protect a fragile self-esteem or a diminished and delusional sense of being unworthy in order to elicit generosity from others—without considering that gratitude is a debt to be repaid. What states of ingratitude get triggered for you, and under what circumstances?

The first psalm in the Hebrew scriptures eloquently describes the restoration and healing of the human spirit that take place when our ingratitude is released:

Blessed are the man and woman
who have grown beyond their greed
and have put an end to their hatred
and no longer nourish illusions.
But they delight in the ways things are
and keep their hearts open, day and night.
They are like trees planted near flowing rivers,
which bear fruit when they are ready.
Their leaves will not fall or wither.
Everything they do will succeed.

Suffering and the Gratitude Portal of Mercy

The Persian poet Rumi wrote, "Suffering is a treasure, for it conceals mercies." For example, within the suffering of illness, the mercy that emerges is the chance to rest and replenish; or the loss of a relationship may contain within it the hidden mercy of reconnecting with oneself, and thus reconnecting with other meaningful aspects of life. Our attitudes of ungratefulness cause us, and those around us, much suffering. When we release them, the gratitude portal of mercy opens wide within. We are able to forgive. We can embody kindness. Merciful actions, whether extended to others or received from them, become fortunate moments for which we are immediately grateful. All acts of mercy produce healing and restore the soul. Offering food or clothing to someone who is homeless, assisting someone who is hurt in an accident, or visiting the elderly in the hospital are all unexpected acts of mercy that help alleviate the suffering of others and spontaneously elicit our own generosity.

"All the world's faiths put suffering at the top of their agenda," as Karen Armstrong writes in her book *The Spiral Staircase*, "because it is an inescapable fact of human life, and unless you see things as they really are, you cannot live correctly. But even more important, if we deny our own pain, it is all too easy to dismiss the suffering of others. Every single one of the major traditions—Confucianism, Buddhism, Hinduism, as well as the monotheisms—teaches a spirituality of empathy, by means of which you relate your own suffering to that of others."

Wherever we find our heart closed, we are being shown the root of our suffering, and we are being invited to be merciful, to forgive, or make amends. Caroline Myss, in her book *Anatomy of the Spirit,* says "When we harbor negative emotions toward others or toward ourselves, or when we intentionally create pain for others, we poison our own physical and spiritual systems. By far the strongest poison to the human spirit is the inability to forgive oneself or another person. It disables a person's emotional resources. The challenge . . . is to refine our capacity to love others as well as ourselves and to develop the power of forgiveness."

Wherever we are closed-hearted, we are holding onto grudges, resentments, and old disappointments. These emotional states can be opportunities to look at where we can become more compassionate with ourselves or others. Or, they are opportunities to review honestly whether or not we are ready to extend mercy or forgiveness, or make amends at this time. If we are not yet ready to do so, can we also forgive ourselves for not letting go of our position? What will alleviate or resolve the suffering that is currently being experienced? What amends or actions are needed? Witnessing how others deal with suffering, or seeing how others release their closed-heartedness, may have the unintended effect of increasing our own gratitude for life, and it may reopen our hearts. Often, the courageous acts and attitudes of others facing adversity inspire our generosity and motivate us to put our petty resentments or self-righteous grudges into proper perspective.

What self-forgiveness work is revealing itself to you at this time? What reparation or act of mercy is needed so you may forgive yourself and others? What is it that you are not yet willing to forgive, and can you forgive yourself for that? Notice what states of ingratitude may be preventing you from receiving or extending mercy and forgiveness to yourself and others.

Sanctifying the Soul: Repentance, Contrition, and Atonement

The traditional themes of resurrection, redemption, and purification that surface this month are invitations to recognize our states of ingratitude and release them. In so doing, we nurture and sanctify the soul. This is not always easy to do; it requires us to consciously move out from the darkness of these harmful states into the light of hope and trust. Spiritual traditions have held that the ways we can break free of darkness are through the practices of forgiveness, repentance, contrition, and atonement.

Many indigenous societies on the North American continent speak of three medicines that we must carry with us every day: the medicine of genuine acknowledgment; the medicine of genuine apology; and the medicine of laughter and joy. All three medicines are necessary for extending healing and mercies toward ourselves and others. All foster the practice of atonement in our lives, the desire and action to make amends or to come back into natural harmony with oneself (at-one-ment). Atonement and repentance maintain and restore trust and discerning hopefulness within the human spirit.

In the Buddhist tradition, chapter forty of the *Avatam-saka Sutra* provides us with a prayer of atonement to reflect upon every day:

> *For all the harmful things I've done, with my body,*
> *speech and mind, from beginningless greed, anger*
> *and stupidity, through lifetimes without number, to*
> *this very day; I now repent and I vow, to change entirely.*

The three major means for making amends are repentance, contrition, and atonement. As a result, we find in all spiritual traditions prayers and invocations that address these three themes, which sanctify and purify the soul. The season of spring offers us the opportunity to come back into our natural state of at-one-ment—both internally and externally—with ourselves and others. And the practice of gratitude is what fosters this increased congruence in our lives.

❧

April's invitation is to sustain hope and trust in life through practices of gratitude and mercy. Healing occurs when the heart is open, trusting, and hopeful—and gratitude creates these environments. When the heart is open, creative solutions and new possibilities are more readily seen, and the mercies within us are more accessible. Spring functions as an irrefutable mirror of human nature's goodness, beauty, and resilience in its ability to survive, grow, and thrive regardless of hardships or injustices.

APRIL BENEFIT OF GRATITUDE-PRACTICE

Did you know that grateful people are more compassionate, merciful, generous, and forgiving? As a result, they are also more hopeful and trusting of themselves, others, and their circumstances. Researcher Robert Emmons also confirms that grateful people are less lonely, bitter, isolated, unforgiving, or indifferent. Barbara Fredrickson, pioneer and researcher in the study of positive emotions, has argued that positive emotions (such as compassion, kindness, empathy, and forgiveness) broaden mindsets and build enduring personal resources. Everett Worthington, in his book *Forgiving and Reconciling: Bridges to Wholeness and Hope,* notices that people who forgive find greater peace and acceptance, and the return of hope fosters more well-being. What triggers your experience of loneliness and isolation? What areas of your life are hopeful? What do you currently trust about yourself and others?

Reflections

*The first principle of non-violent action is that of
non-cooperation with everything humiliating.*

MAHATMA GANDHI

In contemplative practices of any kind, questions provoke
inquiry, reflection, and conscious awareness of what we
are learning or what is being revealed to us about our own
current inner and outer work.

Notice which of the following questions capture your
attention and which are less evocative or interesting to you
at this time. Select two or three of the most meaningful questions for you and explore them more deeply.

- Identify the ingratitude you may be experiencing at work
  and in your relationships. Where are you experiencing
  envy, greed, or jealousy? How are you seeking recognition
  and a sense of self-importance? What triggers your need
  to compare yourself to others? Notice what and who
  takes you to these states of ingratitude.

- What self-forgiveness work is revealing itself at this
  time? What is the reparation work or act of mercy that
  will enable you to forgive yourself and others? What is it
  that you are not yet willing to forgive? Can you forgive
  yourself for that?

- In times when you have experienced suffering or darkness,
  how do you maintain hope and your capacity to trust?

- Look deeply into your suffering for the concealed mercies within it.

- Where are you experiencing the sanctifying and liberating processes of the soul—the presence of mercy and forgiveness in your life?

- What new insights and discoveries have come to you this month about who you are? What essential part of your own nature have you touched that has surprised you or is new to you?

Practices

Practices are essential for integrating what we are learning. Select two or three of the following practices that most specifically apply to your current experience and would help you the most at this time.

- Make amends this month in at least two areas of your life. What actions of repentance and atonement are you ready to take?

- When are you experiencing jealousy, envy, or are comparing yourself to others? Practice strengthening your self-esteem and sense of self-sufficiency by locating yourself consistently in self-trust, self-respect, and remembering your own self-value and unique purpose.

- Recite the verse of the Avatamsaka Sutra at least once every day, or create your own prayer of repentance and atonement.

- Each day during this month, spend an hour in nature and in silence; the soul is strengthened by this practice. Notice what captures your attention and why. What is strengthening within you?

- Give gratitude for the mercies, forgiveness, and repentance that you have extended toward others, as well as for those you have received from others.

- What circumstances or relationships could benefit from the three medicines of genuine acknowledgement, genuine apology, and the fostering of joy, humor, and laughter? Sincerely extend and work with these medicines in your life this month.

- What is your current relationship to faith and trust? Journal or write a page about where faith and trust are strong in your life and where they are currently being tested. How have your faith and trust strengthened this year?

Review and Integration

Gratitude in the Four Quadrants of Life

work

relationships

**SPIRITUAL GROWTH &
DEVELOPING CHARACTER**

finances

health

Notice what you are grateful for in the four quadrants of your life:

- Work/creative service

- Relationships: friends, colleagues, and family

- Finances and right livelihood

- Health and well-being

The center of the four quadrants represents the place of *developing character* and connecting to your own *spiritual growth* and development. The center is influenced, impacted, and informed by all four quadrants. To help you discover the sources of your gratitude, answer the following tracking questions and see which quadrant or quadrants are emphasized more for you this month.

In looking at the illustration of the Four Quadrants of Life, consider the following questions:

- What are you seeing that is similar to last month's work? What is different, or significantly changing? Review the four quadrants of your life. What is being most activated in either your work, relationships, finances, or health?

- What internal insights and discoveries are you making that have strengthened your character and fostered spiritual growth this month?

- What are you noticing that is new, expanded, or being released in each quadrant of your life this month?

- What are you grateful for in each of your life's quadrants, and how are you expressing your thankfulness?

Blessings, Learnings, Mercies, and Protections

Express your gratitude by reflecting upon:

- The major *Blessings* you have given and received during April.

- The major *Learnings* you have given and received during April.

- The major *Mercies* you have given and received during April.

- The major *Protections* you have given and received during April.

The following questions can help you go deeper in your exploration of these four portals to gratitude.

External Questions

- Who or what has inspired you?

- Who or what is challenging you?

- Who or what is surprising you?

- Who or what is touching or moving you?

Internal Questions

- What is strengthening within my nature?

- What is softening within my nature?

- What is opening within my nature?

- What is deepening within my nature?

{ May }

May Prayer

Help us, Oh Lord to remember our kindred

*beyond the sea—all those who bend in bonds,
of our own blood and of human kind—
the lowly and the wretched, the ignorant and the weak.
We are one world . . . and one great human problem
and what we do here goes to solve not only
our petty troubles alone but the difficulties
and desires of millions unborn and unknown.
Let us then realize our responsibilities and
gain strength to bear them worthily.*

W. E. B. Du Bois (1868–1963)

The Gift
of Grace

Pride and grace do not dwell in the same place.

OLD SAYING

THE FIRST DAY of May honors the traditional spring festival of Beltane, when on the British Isles people gather together to dance around a garlanded maypole. Tethered to the pole by colorful ribbons, the dancers encircle it again and again as their ribbons intertwine. This celebratory ancient dance is performed in honor of Maia, the May queen after whom this month is named. The traditional maypole dance itself and the joy of the revelers are physical expressions of gratitude that continue to be passed on from generation to generation.

Maia is the goddess of increase and abundance, qualities that are hallmarks of this month when spring is in its fullness.

In May, nature mirrors back to us the increased blossoming and opening that are also occurring in our lives and within our own natures. We may experience a burst of renewed creativity, the excitement of a new relationship, or a greater intensity of feeling in our physical experience of the world. Perhaps a new dimension of our character suddenly awakens, or our spirit unexpectedly soars to new heights. Any of these experiences might naturally occur at this time of plenty.

Also during the month of May, Mother's Day is celebrated around the world to honor women who are mothers and to give gratitude for the gift of life. This is an ancient practice that invokes the mother archetype and its life-nurturing force. In May, life is full of abundance and we are reminded of the unlimited possibilities that are available to us in nurturing all areas of our life.

Gratitude and Grace

This month we will explore the relationship between gratitude and grace. The two words share the same root from the Latin *grata* or *gratia* (a given gift). The experience of grace evokes the expression of gratitude.

In her book *Attitudes of Gratitude,* M. J. Ryan defines grace as "an experience in which individuals slip out of ordinary space and time, where there is no separation between themselves and the world around them, and everything seems perfect just as it is. Some people find such moments of transcendence through meditation, others in nature, still others when making love or being totally absorbed in work that is meaningful. These moments are rare gifts in which we open to an expansive place within our nature, where all is right with us and the world."

Grace has another meaning connected to gratitude as well. From humankind's earliest beginnings to today, we have "said grace" for the life-giving food we are about to eat or share with others. Worldwide, food continues to be a social and spiritual link to thanksgiving and a universal experience of gratitude.

In the spiritual traditions of the world, grace is considered the divine reality that underlies all faith. In Christian scripture, for example, we find: "From his fullness we have all received grace upon grace" (John 1:16). This is the recognition of the unmerited love of God, or the human experience of a transcendent state that releases us from suffering.

Father Bede Griffiths was the first to bridge Christian practices with Hindu and Buddhist traditions. He identified the *four immeasurables* in Buddhism as comparable to the grace released in the practice of the Eucharist. The four immeasurable graces are compassion, loving-kindness, joy, and equanimity. We express our gratitude more frequently as we become more loving, compassionate, joyful, and accepting of life's rewards and challenges. In Hinduism, grace is found in the love of the Hindu triad: Brahma, Vishnu, and Shiva.

Within the Christian tradition, the Eucharist is the act and practice of thanksgiving. Through the Eucharist we enter into the state of grace as we recognize that all has originated as a gift and generous blessing from God. The destiny and true grace of all creation is inter-communion. This sense of unity, interconnectedness, and belonging accentuates the experience of grace and motivates the expression of gratitude, awe, and wonder within us.

Whether we are religious, spiritual, agnostic, or atheist, we can recognize the state of grace. It is a transcendent experience of unity, peacefulness, and complete trust that brings us back to our common humanity.

Grace and Gratitude Integrated: Developing Gravitas

Also sharing the same root with grace and gratitude is the word *gravitas,* and there is a strong interconnection among these three states. When people internalize and integrate their experience of grace, their character naturally deepens and they develop gravitas. In Latin, *gravitas* is similar to charisma, and is defined as a quality that draws us to those who embody dignity, integrity, wisdom, substance, and presence.

The sixteenth-century saint Teresa of Avila embodied the progression from grace to gratitude to gravitas. She viewed her many mystical experiences as states of grace, and she responded to them with deep gratitude. This, in turn, moved her to serve others, and ultimately, she founded an entire spiritual order. It was the charisma, the gravitas, that had become integrated into her personality that enabled her to accomplish such a momentous task.

Nelson Mandela is a modern-day example of this process. When he was imprisoned on Robben Island, he was a very angry man. During his imprisonment, however, he had many transformational experiences—states of grace—that reshaped him, and he, too, was moved by gratitude to make a difference in the world. *Gravitas* is a word that is often used when describing this influential leader of today.

Being conscious of where grace is present in our lives motivates our expression of gratitude and cultivates gravitas. Gratitude is the external expression of grace and gravitas in our lives. In all of these states we touch our inherent goodness.

The Gift of Silence

While this time of year is one of accentuated activity, it is best balanced with periods of stillness, as the states of grace, gravitas, and gratitude are cultivated and experienced foremost in silence. Thomas Merton speaks of silence as a constant reality that will not fail us:

> The reality that is present to us and in us: call it being
> . . . Silence. And the simple fact that by being attentive,
> by learning to listen (or recovering the natural capacity
> to listen) we can find ourself engulfed in such happiness
> that it cannot be explained: the happiness of being at
> one with everything in that hidden ground of Love for
> which there can be no explanation . . . May we all grow
> in grace and peace, and not neglect the silence that is
> printed in the centre of our beings. It will not fail us.

Give yourself the gift of silence. Allow yourself the opportunity to be still and notice where there is the experience of grace and ease in your life—the awakening, exploring, growing, and responding parts of your nature that remain curious and attentive rather than critical and assessing. These are places of grace. The more time we spend reflecting on these places in silence or meditation, and the more we act on the guidance we receive—thereby integrating the experience—the more we can develop personal gravitas.

A Time to Honor Our Ancestors

Worldwide, every culture honors its ancestors through ritual at some time during the year. Flowers, candles, greenery, and symbols of beauty are always used in one form or another. Such heartfelt offerings are a natural expression of the gratitude we feel for what we have received from those who have passed on. By making the offering at this time of year, we ensure that our appreciation is not limited to what we enjoy in the natural upliftment and grace of spring. We recognize that the gifts we are thankful for today have deep roots in the past.

Ancestor spirits are defined cross-culturally as family members and friends who are no longer living but remain important teachers of detachment. This is because they have faced the process of letting go and have experienced the ultimate unknown: death. Indigenous peoples worldwide believe that these spirits literally stand behind us to support us, with most believing that the male ancestor spirits stand behind us on the right side of the body, and the female ancestor spirits stand behind us on the left. They believe these spirits are invested in seeing that the current generation and those to come can fulfill their dreams, or life purpose. The following European ancestral chant, passed down through oral tradition, clearly states how ancestors may support us:

Oh, may this be the one who
will bring forward
the good, true and beautiful in our
family lineage;
Oh, may this be one who will
break the harmful
family patterns or harmful national
patterns.

In *Tragic Sense of Life,* the Basque philosopher Miguel de Unamuno reminds us of the importance of ancestral connection that is so deeply rooted within us: "All my ancestors live undiminished in me, and will continue so to live, united with me, in my descendants." Many indigenous cultures recognize that each individual is a tradition bearer for the past generation and the generations to come. It is important to consider in what ways we can bring forward the good, true, and beautiful that are carried in our heritage, and to know that the quality of our life contributes to the opportunities and challenges of future generations.

For Americans, May brings Memorial Day, a national holiday reminding us to honor those who have died in war, as well as to honor veterans who have survived. The courage of these heroes and heroines reminds us of the inherent grace that comes from feeling safe and protected. Todd Kashdan, an assistant professor at George Mason University and director of the Laboratory for the Study of Social Anxiety, Character Strength, and Related Phenomena, has found that the practice of gratitude significantly increased the emotional comfort and well-being of Vietnam War veterans. Memorial Day is essentially a national holiday that sets aside time to offer gratitude for the great gift of life itself. In doing so we collectively increase our own well-being, whether we are conscious of it or not.

Aboriginal Rites of Gratitude

We can learn much about honoring the ancestors from the Australian Aborigines. The deep spiritual connection the Aborigines have to their land and their ancestral beings is well known. Aborigines conduct both seasonal and daily rituals of gratitude to honor the ancestors, trusting that these ceremonies will protect their land and the people who walk upon it today. The Dreamtime is at the very core of the Aborigines' belief system surrounding spiritual and worldly abundance, and they believe the ancestral beings perform wondrous deeds from the Dreamtime to help transform this world. They trust that these beings will continue to support the beauty and bounty of the land if the living sing daily songs of praise to the ancestral water holes, to the places where food is plentiful, and to sacred story sites. These rites will protect the spirits of land and place and those now living on the ancestral lands.

The tradition of reenacting the events of the Dreamtime through ritual and ceremony is passed on from generation to generation. If it were not, the Dreamtime would stop and the world would end. Those performing the rites become Dreamtime beings and are able to tap the power of the land and the ancestors. Through oral traditions, body paintings, dances, songs, and enactments of ancient stories, the Aborigines maintain a deep connection to their roots and the world around them.

Who are the ancestors and loved ones you pay tribute to each year? In what ways does your family honor its ancestors after they are gone? Which ones had a strong relationship to nature, silence, and abundance? Which of your ancestors embodied grace, gratitude, and gravitas?

Nine Principles from Japan

The quality of grace that is associated with Maia also appears in Japan at this time of year. There, spring is the season to manifest beauty and demonstrate success that comes from excellence and grace, rather than from perfection and pride. In *The Book of Five Rings,* Miyamoto Musashi, the famed samurai, says that there are nine principles one can practice and embody to achieve the success that comes with grace and excellence as follows:

- Do not harbor sinister designs.

- Diligently pursue the Path of Two-Swords-as-One (the Middle Way).

- Cultivate a wide range of interests in the arts.

- Be knowledgeable in a variety of occupations.

- Be discreet regarding one's commercial dealings.

- Nurture the ability to perceive the truth in all things.

- Perceive that which cannot be seen with the eye.

- Do not be negligent in trifling matters.

- Do not engage in useless activity.

Which of these nine principles are the most developed and least developed for you in your life right now? For example, is appreciation for art a part of your daily life at this time? Are there minor tasks that could benefit from increased attention? Have you recently broadened your knowledge into new areas? How much beauty and excellence are you currently bringing into your life? What aspects of perfectionistic striving or overcompensating pride need to be released from your life and your own nature at this time? May's invitation is to restore our inherent beauty and excellence. Will we seize this opportunity?

❧

This month offers rich opportunities to both celebrate and commemorate, to be creative, to sit in stillness, to revel in the beauty of the present, and to connect to and honor the past. Above all, May is a time of grace, a quality that places us well along on our journey toward living in gratitude.

MAY BENEFIT OF GRATITUDE-PRACTICE

What does modern research tell us about the link between gratitude and religion or spirituality? People who describe themselves as either religious or spiritual are more likely to be grateful than those who describe themselves as neither. "A Gallup survey reported that 54 percent of adults and 37 percent of teens said they express thanks to God or Creator 'all of the time.' Two-thirds of those surveyed said they express gratitude to God by saying grace before meals, and three out of four reported expressing thanks to God through worship or prayer."

There is a fundamental spiritual quality to gratitude that transcends religious traditions. Gratitude is a universal human experience that can seem to be either a random occurrence of grace or a chosen attitude to create a better experience of life; in many ways it contains elements of both. Grateful people sense that they are not separated from others or from God; this recognition of unity with all things brings a deep sense of gratefulness, whether we are religious or not.

Reflections

Virtue is bold and goodness never fearful.

SHAKESPEARE, FROM *MEASURE FOR MEASURE*

In contemplative practices of any kind, questions provoke inquiry, reflection, and conscious awareness of what we are learning or what is being revealed to us about our own current inner and outer work.

Notice which of the following questions capture your attention and which are less evocative or interesting to you at this time. Select two or three of the most meaningful questions for you and explore them more deeply.

- Notice and give gratitude for all that makes you happy and brings joy into your life.

- What experiences of grace have you had this month? What is your own experience of the relationship between grace, gravitas, and gratitude?

- In what ways do you give gratitude to your mother? What is nurturing and life-giving to you at this time, and in what ways are you nurturing and life-giving to others?

- Where are you experiencing beauty and excellence in your life?

- Review Mushashi's nine principles to achieve success that comes with grace. What are you discovering and learning in relationship to these nine principles?

- What are you learning about what Merton calls "the happiness of being one with everything," the "hidden ground of Love"? What triggers these experiences for you?

Practices

Practices are essential for integrating what we are learning. Select two or three of the following practices that most specifically apply to your current experience and would help you the most at this time.

- During this month, track and give gratitude for the places of grace and peace in your life, and within your own nature. What is awakening, growing, and increasing in your life?

- Spend at least a half hour in silent mediation every day to deeply listen to the "centre of [your] being. It will not fail [you]."

- During the month of May, strengthen your character and excellence in leadership by taking a day and working with one of Mushashi's nine principles.

- What practices do you have that honor your ancestors and loved ones who have gone before you? Like the traditions of the Australian Aborigines, what are the songs, stories, and family rituals that have been passed down through the generations? What new rituals or traditions are you creating for your family to remember and honor the ancestors?

- Seek out your family genealogy as a way of honoring your ancestral lineages and heritage. Develop a daily practice of gratitude by honoring your ancestors and calling upon them for support as you make changes in your life.

- Write a poem, prayer, or story about when grace and gratitude together presented themselves to you in a life experience.

- Create a gratitude study group that meets monthly to work with this or other related books.

Review and Integration

Gratitude in the Four Quadrants of Life

work   relationships

**SPIRITUAL GROWTH &
DEVELOPING CHARACTER**

finances   health

Notice what you are grateful for in the four quadrants of your life:

- Work/creative service

- Relationships: friends, colleagues, and family

- Finances and right livelihood

- Health and well-being

The center of the four quadrants represents the place of *developing character* and connecting to your own *spiritual growth* and development. The center is influenced, impacted, and informed by all four quadrants. To help you discover the sources of your gratitude, answer the following tracking questions and see which quadrant or quadrants are emphasized more for you this month.

In looking at the illustration of the Four Quadrants of Life, consider the following questions:

- What are you seeing that is similar to last month's work? What is different, or significantly changing? Review the four quadrants of your life. What is being most activated in either your work, relationships, finances, or health?

- What internal insights and discoveries are you making that have strengthened your character and fostered spiritual growth this month?

- What are you noticing that is new, expanded, or being released in each quadrant of your life this month?

- What are you grateful for in each of your life's quadrants, and how are you expressing your thankfulness?

Blessings, Learnings, Mercies, and Protections

blessings

mercies   protections

learnings

Express your gratitude by reflecting upon:

- The major *Blessings* you have given and received during May.

- The major *Learnings* you have given and received during May.

- The major *Mercies* you have given and received during May.

- The major *Protections* you have given and received during May.

The following questions can help you go deeper in your exploration of these four portals to gratitude.

External Questions

- Who or what has inspired you?

- Who or what is challenging you?

- Who or what is surprising you?

- Who or what is touching or moving you?

Internal Questions

- What is strengthening within my nature?

- What is softening within my nature?

- What is opening within my nature?

- What is deepening within my nature?

{ June }

June Prayer

Judaic Prayer of Thanks

*Throughout all generations
we will render thanks unto Thee*

and declare Thy praise,

Evening, morning and noon,

For our lives which are in Thy care,

For our souls which are in Thy keeping

For Thy miracles which we witness daily,

*And for Thy wondrous deeds and blessings
toward us at all times.*

JEWISH SABBATH PRAYER

The Power of
Equanimity

Give thanks for a little and you will find a lot.

HAUSA PROVERB FROM NIGERIA

PEOPLE AROUND THE world observe spiritual and religious celebrations during the month of June. Most of these center on holy days that are linked to the summer solstice. In the Northern Hemisphere at solstice time, on or around June twenty-first, daytime hours are at their longest and nighttime hours at their shortest, and the abundance of sunlight marks the first day of summer. This day is also referred to as Midsummer, because it is roughly in the middle of the growing season throughout much of Europe.

In prehistoric times in the northern latitudes, summer was a joyous time of year for the aboriginal people who lived there. The snow had disappeared, the ground had thawed, and warm temperatures had returned. Flowers bloomed and deciduous trees were covered in new leaves. Most societies in the Northern Hemisphere, ancient and modern, have celebrated a festival on or close to Midsummer, an event Shakespeare drew upon for his play *A Midsummer Night's Dream*.

The month of June is named after the Roman goddess Juno, who was married to Jupiter, the god of abundance and growth in all areas of our lives. Juno was the goddess of marriage who recognized meaningful and committed love.

Light, Fire, and the Kindling of Love

The summer solstice is a time of light and fire. With the persistent sun beckoning all life to come into its own, it is a time to reflect upon the growth now taking place within ourselves and within nature. June is the midpoint of the year, and it affords us the opportunity to course-correct if need be, now that we can see the vivid expression of the seeds we have sown in the earth, as well as those that have been planted in our hearts and souls.

Often, June reveals to us what continues to be deeply meaningful for us in our work and family life. The beginning of summer mirrors back to us what is fulfilling, renewing, and nurturing to us—and what is not. What is not tolerated at this time is any situation in our work or relationships that has become a "should," where we feel duty-bound. Whatever is not aligned or congruent with our integrity and heart is forced to be released at the midpoint of the year, or reassessed in its meaning to us. The symbol most associated with summer is fire. In its constructive forms, fire allows us to burn or let go of our "shoulds" and realign with the fire of the heart and what is most meaningful and renewing to us.

The solstice is also a time of romantic love, a reflection of fiery energy. In ancient Europe, Midsummer was celebrated with bonfires. It was a time for consulting love oracles for predictions, to see if one's love was star-crossed or not. Romantic pairs jumped over fires together for luck, with the belief that both their love and the crops that were now growing would grow as high as the couples were able to jump.

Juno's month has long been the traditional month of weddings, and it remains a favorite time for marriage ceremonies today. Every culture has ritualized marriage. In some traditions, for the first month of their married life, newlywed couples were fed dishes and beverages that featured honey, a practice meant to encourage love and fertility. If the wedding took place in June, the timing for this would be perfect: the full moon in June is called "the honey moon," so named because tradition holds that it is the best time to harvest beehives. The surviving vestige of this tradition lives on in the name given to the holiday couples take immediately after their wedding.

Balance, Equanimity, and Renewal

In ancient China, the summer solstice celebrated the earth, the feminine, and yin forces. This complemented the winter solstice, which celebrated the heavens, masculinity, and yang forces. The balance of yin and yang forces is considered essential in Asian societies as a way to be most effective in work and relationships. Twice a year these balance points are reconsidered, first at the winter solstice and again at the summer solstice. It is believed that in states of balance, we can renew ourselves. Yoshimoto Ishin, a member of the Jodo Shinshu sect in Japan, developed a Buddhist meditation technique called Naikan, a self-reflection process consisting of three questions designed to cultivate gratitude and help us see the reciprocal quality of relationships:

- What have I received from _____?

- What have I given to_____?

- What troubles and difficulties have I caused _____?

At the midpoint of the year, these questions help us address issues in relationships, work situations, social interactions, and in developing the higher aspects of ourselves. The first question helps us recognize all the gifts we receive and the good that comes to us every day. The second question helps us develop compassion and shows us how and why we are connected to other people. The last question acknowledges where we cause pain or suffering in the lives of others by our thoughts, words, and deeds.

Gregg Krech, who wrote on the practice of Naikan, addresses the challenge of this last question: "If we are not willing to see and accept those events in which we have been the source of others' suffering, then we cannot truly know ourselves or the grace by which we live." The practice of Naikan strengthens and restores the balance of giving and receiving in all our relationships. It not only cultivates gratitude but reinstates equanimity.

The month of June is a time of growth and fullness. It is an opportunity for all living things to grow and integrate the magnetic (yin) and dynamic (yang) forces within their natures. In summer, what is out of balance is pulled back into balance. Perhaps that is why in summer, particularly after the solstice, we have the modern practice of taking a vacation—*vacating* or stepping out of our daily routine in order to integrate our experiences. Summer offers a time to renew our creativity and gain new perspectives. It is natural to ask ourselves: What is coming to fullness and growing within our life or heart at this year's midpoint? What is out of balance and needs to be rebalanced or course-corrected in our life this year?

June offers a month to practice equanimity: the experience of nothing lacking and of accepting all things as they are. Equanimity is the state of mental and emotional stability and composure arising from a deep awareness and acceptance of the present moment. For example, Patrick O'Neill, president of Extraordinary Conversations, Inc., reminds us that an important threshold in leadership is reached when a leader begins to embody the aspect of equanimity that "can meet disturbance without disturbance," especially in conflictual situations. This quality of equanimity is also valued and promoted by many spiritual traditions worldwide. In Hinduism, equanimity is a concept of balance and centeredness that endures through all possible changes and circumstances. In Buddhism, equanimity is a state of neutrality that is without hostility or ill will. Judaic scholars highlight the importance of equanimity as a necessary foundation for moral and spiritual development. The word *Islam* is derived from the Arabic word *aslama,* which denotes the peace that comes from total surrender and acceptance. Being a Muslim can therefore be understood to mean that one is in a state of equanimity. In Christian philosophy, equanimity is considered essential for carrying out the virtues of gentleness, temperance, and charity. Taoist philosopher Lao-tzu describes equanimity as a way of living.

In summer, nature mirrors back to us where we are experiencing equanimity and where we are not. In June, reflect daily on the following words of Lao-tzu as you practice equanimity as a way of living:

If you look to others for fulfillment
you will never be truly fulfilled.
If your happiness depends on money,
you will never be happy with yourself.

Be content with what you have;
rejoice in the way things are.
When you realize nothing is lacking,
the whole world belongs to you.

The state of equanimity opens us to the disposition of gratefulness and allows us to see more of the blessings in our lives. We experience equanimity, or a sense of balance, when we are content with the way things are. We are neither striving nor holding back. There is nothing lacking or in excess. This balance, or sense of acceptance, is at the heart of equanimity. It opens us to the experience of gratitude and the sustainable experience of renewal that comes from being in balance.

Opportunities to live daily in gratitude surface abundantly during this month when summer begins. The seeds we have planted have sprouted. The sun's enduring fire sparks what has heart and meaning for us and is expressed through rituals and celebrations. Balancing at the midpoint of the year, we have an opportunity to regain our equanimity. These are gifts we can receive in June if we open ourselves to them, and each is its own catalyst for appreciation and thankfulness.

JUNE: BENEFIT OF GRATITUDE-PRACTICE

According to Robert Emmons, "The significance of gratitude lies in its ability . . . to enrich human life. Gratitude elevates, it energizes, it inspires, it transforms. People are moved, opened, and humbled through experiences and expressions of gratitude. Gratitude provides life with meaning by encapsulating life itself as a gift. Without gratitude, life can be lonely, depressing, impoverished."

Edward Diener, the father of happiness research, and Martin Seligman, the father of positive psychology, conducted a study in 2002 focusing on two groups of people: those with the highest scores on a standard measure of happiness and those with the lowest. They discovered that "the one trait the happy group had in common, which the unhappy group didn't share, was having close, trusting relationships and more balance and harmony in their lives."

Reflections

O that you were yourself.

SHAKESPEARE, SONNET 13

In contemplative practices of any kind, questions provoke inquiry, reflection, and conscious awareness of what we are learning or what is being revealed to us about our own current inner and outer work.

Notice which of the following questions capture your attention and which are less evocative or interesting to you at this time. Select two or three of the most meaningful questions for you and explore them more deeply.

- What are you discovering about the places of balance and imbalance in your life at this midpoint of the year? What new insights have surfaced for you? Where is it difficult for you to maintain balance in your life?

- What is your current relationship to equanimity? As you read and reread Lao-tzu's passage about equanimity and acceptance, what are you discovering? What is difficult for you to accept?

- What is surfacing in your relationships at this time? Relationships mirror back to us what is easy or challenging about giving and receiving, and what is acceptable or not acceptable (issues surrounding our limits and boundaries). They reveal to us which of the forces of magnetism (yin energy) and forces of dynamism (yang energy) we are more comfortable expressing. Is it more comfortable to give (yang) or receive (yin) in your relationships?

- What difficulties, challenges, or harm are you experiencing or causing in your relationships at this time?

- How are you "meeting disturbance without disturbance"? This is an important aspect of equanimity.

- Who or what do you love or feel passionately about at this time?

- June is nature's time of growing, of coming to fullness. Growing requires us to come out of our comfort zones. Where are you growing in your life? What is coming to fullness?

- Where are you experiencing increasing congruence and alignment with what is truly meaningful and important to you?

Practices

Practices are essential for integrating what we are learning. Select two or three of the following practices that most specifically apply to your current experience and would help you the most at this time.

- Find out as much as you can about the principle of equanimity. What does it mean to you? Invite others to join you and host an evening's conversation to explore equanimity and its relationship to gratitude.

- For one week, track the triggers that you let take you off balance or into states of reactivity, denial, or indulgence. In what ways do you bring yourself back into balance when you are off balance?

- Spending time in silence cultivates and strengthens our connection to the sense of peacefulness and acceptance that is available to us in states of equanimity. Set aside a half hour each day to sit or walk in silence. Notice what is revealed to you in the silence—especially the solace and peaceful moments it offers you.

- Continue every day to do the practice of Naikan to improve your relationships. Spend a half hour reviewing the three relationship questions from the Japanese art of Naikan, and take at least one positive action each day to improve your relationships at home and at work.

- What internal and external means do you have to promote and support the areas in which you are growing? Identify them and add a related action to your practice.

- Celebrate and give gratitude for at least three things that are working very well in your life at this time.

Review and Integration

Gratitude in the Four Quadrants of Life

work   relationships

SPIRITUAL GROWTH & DEVELOPING CHARACTER

finances   health

Notice what you are grateful for in the four quadrants of your life:

- Work/creative service

- Relationships: friends, colleagues, and family

- Finances and right livelihood

- Health and well-being

The center of the four quadrants represents the place of *developing character* and connecting to your own *spiritual growth* and development. The center is influenced, impacted, and informed by all four quadrants. To help you discover the sources of your gratitude, answer the following tracking questions and see which quadrant or quadrants are emphasized more for you this month.

In looking at the illustration of the Four Quadrants of Life, consider the following questions:

- What are you seeing that is similar to last month's work? What is different, or significantly changing? Review the four quadrants of your life. What is being most activated in either your work, relationships, finances, or health?

- What internal insights and discoveries are you making that have strengthened your character and fostered spiritual growth this month?

- What are you noticing that is new, expanded, or being released in each quadrant of your life this month?

- What are you grateful for in each of your life's quadrants, and how are you expressing your thankfulness?

Blessings, Learnings, Mercies, and Protections

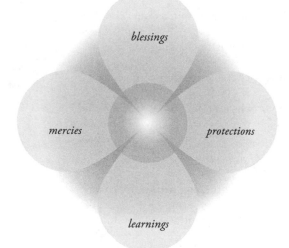

Express your gratitude by reflecting upon:

- The major *Blessings* you have given and received during June.

- The major *Learnings* you have given and received during June.

- The major *Mercies* you have given and received during June.

- The major *Protections* you have given and received during June.

The following questions can help you go deeper in your exploration of these four portals to gratitude.

External Questions

- Who or what has inspired you?

- Who or what is challenging you?

- Who or what is surprising you?

- Who or what is touching or moving you?

Internal Questions

- What is strengthening within my nature?

- What is softening within my nature?

- What is opening within my nature?

- What is deepening within my nature?

{ July }

July Prayer

A Grace Before Dinner

O Thou, who kindly dost provide

For ev'ry creature's want!

We bless Thee, God of Nature wide,

For all Thy goodness lent:

And if it please Thee, Heavenly Guide,

May never be worse be sent;

But, whether granted or denied,

Lord, bless us with content.

ROBERT BURNS (1759–1796)

Embracing
Nature

Love the world as your self;
then you can care for all things.

TAO TE CHING

JULY IS THE month that honors Julius Caesar, who introduced the Julian calendar in 46 BC. Prior to this reform, the year ran from March to March. The new calendar began in January and ended in December, and ever since this is how we have marked the passing of the seasons. Now, at this midpoint of our standard Julian calendar, we embark upon the second half of our journey toward living in gratitude.

In the United States, Americans observe the Fourth of July in celebration of the 1776 Declaration of Independence, our foundational document for democratic governance. This is a day of honoring our freedoms and civil rights, when we can reflect on our own independence and how we foster the spirit of self-sufficiency and freedom within ourselves and others. The holiday affords us an opportunity to appreciate the best aspects of these qualities.

Nature's Laws of Governance

In contrast to the underlying principle of our Fourth of July tradition, nature reflects its own natural laws of governance, asserting a "declaration of interdependence." Mother Nature governs herself in three ways: (1) everything in nature is constantly creating and diversifying; (2) everything has a purpose for its existence; and (3) everything coexists and fosters the principle of interdependence. Since we are also creatures of nature, we, too, innately relate to these principles. We have a basic need and instinct to create, to apply our gifts and talents in new and innovative ways in order to manifest something new. We all have our own purpose and reason for being here, whether we discover it early in life, late, or not at all, and whether we choose to fulfill it or not. And while freedom and independence are available for us to exercise, our gifts and talents can only flourish within the principle of interdependence. Nothing survives in nature if it is fiercely independent or excessively dependent. The heart of interdependence requires collaboration and reciprocity.

We can benefit greatly from observing nature's laws through the eyes of others. In his last book, *The Wisdom of the Wilderness,* renowned psychologist Gerald May describes how nature replenished him and provided comfort during the final year of his life. He felt an interconnectedness and mutual reciprocity that he found holy and transcendent. Poet Mary Oliver writes about her daily encounters with nature; much of her writing is filled with gratitude for what she has been privileged to learn from and witness. She poignantly describes the insights she has gathered from nature that can be applied to her life and relationships, capturing the beauty and blessing of nature as well as her deep appreciation for these encounters. When have you felt a sense of mutual reciprocity as Gerald May found in his experience of the natural world? When have you been filled with gratitude while in natural environments, as Mary Oliver has? When has the power of nature helped you gain clarity about your purpose and how you might apply your gifts and talents in new ways? These are some of nature's gifts.

Four Natural Qualities for Survival

In the natural world, *keen attention, flexibility, resourcefulness,* and *patience* are the four qualities needed to ensure survival. Animals, birds, water creatures, reptiles, plants, trees, and mountains all demonstrate these qualities in both subtle and dramatic ways. Many traditional societies prepare their children for attending to the natural world by giving them the responsibility for taking care of a plant or an animal, which also serves as preparation for attending to human relationships. This practice requires children to discover within themselves and develop the essential four qualities that enable myriad life forms to survive together naturally and interdependently. In caring for a plant or an animal, we need to be resourceful, patient, and flexible and remain keenly attentive to what it needs in the moment; only then can it continue to flourish. These same four qualities are needed to cultivate our own personal growth and development. Just as we would not withdraw what a plant or animal needs to ensure vibrant life, it is important for us to remain equally attentive and nurturing to our own growth processes so that we too can continue to flourish.

For the month of July, develop within your nature the qualities needed for survival in the natural world. Notice what changes, and the opportunities these qualities bring to your home and work environments. The more we spend time in the wild places and the better we care for our natural environments, the more skillfully we can attend to the interior wilderness within us. Begin by noticing during this month what aspects of nature you deeply love.

The Book of Job tells us, "Speak to the Earth and it shall teach thee." Native Americans also believe that the natural world teaches us not only about our own nature, but about interdependence in relationship to our life's purpose. From this belief is born the vision quest, when individuals spend an extended time alone in nature to better understand both the internal and external work before them and learn to care for their inner and outer nature. What expanded vision of yourself do you seek? Do you feel moved to strike out into the natural world on your own? Where would you go, and how would you prepare?

Today there are many wilderness schools that can prepare us to explore the wild places alone. One that is well
known is Outward Bound, a nonprofit organization that
serves people of all ages and backgrounds by providing active
learning expeditions into nature. These excursions help
people expand the four essential survival skills that nature
so clearly models and teaches. In wilderness settings, people
across the country experience adventure, self-discovery,
and challenge, and they come to realize that they are more
capable and competent than they thought or imagined.
Discovering nature's power to renew and strengthen, participants consistently report more self-trust, less fear, and a
greater desire to spend solo time in the outdoors. All have
been grateful for the experience, and the majority of them
have felt transformed, imbued with a new desire to persevere
in their wilderness experience, and protect the wild places
that are still available to us.

How much time do you spend outdoors and in nature?
How developed are your capacities for survival and attending
to the survival of the natural world? Has your awareness of
the interdependence of all living beings been integrated into
your actions?

Caring for the Earth

The Earth comes into its full abundance and beauty in
summer, beckoning us to do our part in caring for it. A
line from a Jewish prayer reminds us of our responsibility as stewards of this extraordinary planet: "And He said:

This is a beautiful world that I have given you. Take care of it; do not ruin it." In what ways do we take care of the beautiful world that has been given to us? Whatever we give our keen attention to, or extend resourcefulness toward, will flourish. Where we experience flexibility and patience is where we can extend resilience and humility. These conditions foster openness, which allows us to be more thankful for the extraordinary gift we have been given—the planet Earth.

To illustrate how many people and organizations worldwide have been moved to attend to the Earth's sustainability and majestic beauty, Paul Hawken, author and social entrepreneur, developed an online network called Wiser Earth. The network has quantified the global movement, which consists of 112,000 socially responsible organizations in 243 countries, territories, and sovereign lands working toward environmental sustainability, indigenous rights, and social justice. Wiser Earth sponsors the world's largest free and editable international directory of nongovernmental and socially responsible organizations that collaborate, share knowledge, and build alliances to support the environmental sustainability of water, rain forests, endangered species, and more. Now is a good time to think of the virtually limitless opportunities that lie before us to participate in this global movement to honor and preserve the natural world. As you observe the natural world around you, are you moved to address a need that has yet to find a champion?

Retrieving the Soul

In many cultures it is believed that when we have lost our connection to ourselves and are in states of depression, we need only go to one of four places in nature to retrieve ourselves: the mountains, the deep forests, the waters (lakes, streams, oceans), or the deserts. These four environments provide opportunities for a deeper remembrance of who we are. Returning to nature to find oneself again is often referred to as "soul retrieval work." Which of these environments has provided or continues to provide the most solace for you? Which do you love the most? These favorite or chosen environments draw forth our gratitude and deep thankfulness. They are places where memory and imagination are together reawakened and the lost parts of our nature are brought home again.

Reversing the Nature Deficit

In a single generation, because of the use of computers and social networking, children do not spend much time in nature, and they suffer for this lack of connection to the natural world. Adults are not immune from this; we too are experiencing what psychologists and teachers have identified as nature deficit disorder, which is the subject of Richard Louv's book *Last Child of the Woods: Saving Our Children from Nature Deficit Disorder.* The estrangement from nature that today's wired generation experiences has created some disturbing trends, such as an increase in obesity, attention deficit disorders, and depression. We do not need to succumb to these trends. Louv offers practical, simple solutions to heal the broken bond, and for many of these solutions, we need look no further than our own backyards. Whether we plant a single primrose or a small tree or create an entire garden, our time spent outdoors allows us to discover the birds, butterflies, bees, and wild animals. Even in fairly urban areas, we might find deer, squirrels, raccoons, possums, skunks, mice, and rabbits. Relating to nature's creatures teaches us about the interdependence found between and among all living things. And while we are enjoying the presence of birds and animals and the smell of the earth, we are enhancing our health. Human beings need to be outdoors for one full hour every day in order to maintain health and well-being; natural light and air are that important.

What will you do to experience nature in your own backyard, or perhaps a nearby park, on a daily basis? How will you take care of the beautiful worlds that have been given to you, both the world inside you and the world without? What laws of nature will you adhere to regarding your own purpose, creativity, and fostering of interdependence? These laws are containers that maintain interdependence and allow a healthy expression of self-sufficiency.

❧

July is a month in which to embrace nature, to observe its principles and integrate them into our lives. Attending to the natural world immediately deepens our experience of gratitude. We are grateful when we bear witness to nature's infinite beauty. We marvel at the creativity, purpose, and interdependence we find in every life form. Natural places have the power to heal our very souls, and we cannot help but accept this gift beyond measure with thankful hearts.

JULY BENEFIT OF GRATITUDE-PRACTICE

As we have seen, spending time in nature, in natural light and natural air, is essential for physical and emotional health. This is true for both children and adults, and it gives us a touchstone to gratitude. In his book *The Gift*, Lewis Hyde writes that throughout history, human beings have had some sense that it is wrong to reap the wealth of nature without giving gratitude or making an offering in return for the abundance supplied by Earth. What experience in nature has triggered your extension of gratitude?

Reflections

A bird does not sing because it has an answer. It sings because it has a song.

Maya Angelou

In contemplative practices of any kind, questions provoke inquiry, reflection, and conscious awareness of what we are learning or what is being revealed to us about our own current inner and outer work.

Notice which of the following questions capture your attention and which are less evocative or interesting to you at this time. Select two or three of the most meaningful questions for you and explore them more deeply.

- In what ways do you foster interdependence in your life? Nothing that is fiercely independent or excessively dependent survives in nature. During this month, wean yourself away from these two extreme patterns that impede human nature's capacity for increased flexibility and for fostering interdependence. How will you demonstrate or initiate more cooperation, collaboration, and reciprocity in your life?

- Of the four major places in nature that provide opportunities for soul-retrieval work—the mountains, deep forests, water (rivers, lakes, oceans), and deserts—which are you the most grateful for at this time, and why? How have your preferences for these four major environments changed for you over the years, and why?

- Which of the four survival qualities do you need to develop: keen attention, resourcefulness, flexibility, or patience?

- What obstacles to maintaining a grateful attitude or thankful disposition are you experiencing at this time, if any?

- What is your current relationship to nature? If you are a parent, how are you fostering your child's relationship to nature at this time?

- Review the three laws of Mother Nature's governance at the beginning of the chapter. In what ways is your life congruent with how nature manages herself? In what specific ways are you caring for the Earth?

Practices

Practices are essential for integrating what we are learning. Select two or three of the following practices that most specifically apply to your current experience and would help you the most at this time.

- Each week, take a resourceful action that supports tending to the natural environment—the beautiful world that has been given to us. In small or large ways, make a difference for increased ecological sustainability.

- Practice patience. Impatience is signaled by the instinctive desire to push or hold back. When these impulses emerge, wait and trust. We harm or may even ruin what is naturally emerging when we act prematurely or withhold an action that is needed. Notice what or who triggers your patience or impatience this month.

- Pray daily for the Earth and all your relations.

- Spend a full hour outdoors every day to increase your health and well-being. As creatures of nature, we need natural light and air to support our health. The more quality time we spend in nature, the more we get in touch with our internal nature.

- Create a Nature Journal. As you explore the outdoors, record the animals, birds, insects, flowers, and trees that you see. Keep a log of your favorite places. Notice what keeps capturing your imagination in the natural world. Whatever we pay attention to has meaning for us.

- Form your own group of Earth Keepers to meet monthly and work on environmental sustainability issues in your community. Have a monthly project that helps make a difference in increasing nature's well-being.

- Form a community-based group that wants to learn about shared leadership, cooperation, collaboration, and reciprocity. We all need to work together more collaboratively to solve the problems we face.

- Give gratitude for what you have learned from nature this month, or from what has been strengthened in your own nature this month.

Review and Integration

Gratitude in the Four Quadrants of Life

Notice what you are grateful for in the four quadrants of your life:

- Work/creative service

- Relationships: friends, colleagues, and family

- Finances and right livelihood

- Health and well-being

The center of the four quadrants represents the place of *developing character* and connecting to your own *spiritual growth* and development. The center is influenced, impacted, and informed by all four quadrants. To help you discover the sources of your gratitude, answer the following tracking questions and see which quadrant or quadrants are emphasized more for you this month.

In looking at the illustration of the Four Quadrants of Life, consider the following questions:

- What are you seeing that is similar to last month's work? What is different, or significantly changing? Review the four quadrants of your life. What is being most activated in either your work, relationships, finances, or health?

- What internal insights and discoveries are you making that have strengthened your character and fostered spiritual growth this month?

- What are you noticing that is new, expanded, or being released in each quadrant of your life this month?

- What are you grateful for in each of your life's quadrants, and how are you expressing your thankfulness?

Blessings, Learnings, Mercies, and Protections

Express your gratitude by reflecting upon:

- The major *Blessings* you have given and received during July.

- The major *Learnings* you have given and received during July.

- The major *Mercies* you have given and received during July.

- The major *Protections* you have given and received during July.

The following questions can help you go deeper in your exploration of these four portals to gratitude.

External Questions

- Who or what has inspired you?

- Who or what is challenging you?

- Who or what is surprising you?

- Who or what is touching or moving you?

Internal Questions

- What is strengthening within my nature?

- What is softening within my nature?

- What is opening within my nature?

- What is deepening within my nature?

{ August }

August Prayer

Oh God, you are Peace.

From you comes Peace,

to you returns Peace.

Revive us with a salutation of Peace,

and lead us to your abode of Peace.

A SAYING FROM THE PROPHET,
USED IN DAILY PRAYER BY MUSLIMS

Cultivating Peace

I vow to offer joy to one person in the morning,
and to help relieve the grief of one person
in the afternoon.
I vow to live simply and sanely with few possessions,
and to keep my body healthy.
I vow to let go of all worries and anxiety
in order to be light and free.

PLUM VILLAGE CHANTING AND RECITATION BOOK

AUGUST IS THE month when, in the Northern Hemisphere, summer reaches its zenith and its "august" nature is on full display. The word *august* has several related meanings: marked by grandeur or dignity, inspiring awe and reverence, and commanding respect because of age or character. Those who are courageous, life-enhancing, fair-minded, and honorable become august, and they earn our reverence. Through their presence, they are able to model these qualities for others and inspire them to do what is right in the face of injustice. Where are you currently experiencing awe and reverence in your life? This is a good time to consider who or what is igniting these states for you and stirring you to come into your own dignity and august nature.

The Talmud, a sacred text from the Judaic tradition, teaches that at the time of our death, "the first question asked at the Throne of Judgment is not about belief or ritual, but 'Have you dealt honorably, faithfully in all your dealings with your fellow-man?'" (Talmud, *Shabbat* 31a). The other question that is asked at the Throne of Judgment comes from a vision given to a Judaic wise man, Zusia. He saw that after his death he would be asked, "Zusia, while you were alive, why weren't you Zusia?" This powerful vision so transformed him that he asked others to consider the same question, using their own names, as a form of preparation for when they, too, would be asked.

The first question from the Talmud addresses our integrity in dealing with others. The Zusia question makes us aware of whether we are being ourselves or are instead performing or pretending to be other than who we are; it asks us why we are doing this, reminding us to be fully ourselves. Each of these teachings is a call for personal integrity—a quality that resonates with the sacred art of thanking and blessing.

Lessons of St. Augustine

This month, we are reminded of Augustine of the Roman province Numidia. Better known as St. Augustine, he was a man of the theological world who inspired awe and reverence wherever he went. Born in 354 AD, he lived to be seventy-six years old—remarkable for his time. Early in his long life, he married, had a son, and studied rhetoric, specializing in philosophy and theology. Then, after a sudden conversion experience and ordination, he devoted the next thirty-five years of his life as the Bishop of Hippo Regius (in present day Algeria). He dedicated nearly all of his energies to influencing education, teaching, and prolific writing to promote the Catholic Church in northern Africa, developing a monastery that was eventually recognized as an outstanding theological and training seminary of its time. Many who studied there later became bishops and saints, speaking of Augustine's teachings wherever they went. His work later influenced not only Christian thinking but much of western thought and reasoning.

At the crux of his philosophy, handed down through the centuries, are the practical ideals of humility, mercy, tolerance, and respect for diversity of religious thought and other cultures. His teachings continue to inspire theologians and the secular world today because they reflect a deep commitment to respect everything and everyone, in all that we do.

In taking Augustine's messages to heart, we gain access to all four portals to gratitude. Humility is a blessing, as it allows us to reach beyond ourselves and appreciate the gifts others bring to the world, a natural source of gratitude. His message of mercy opens the generous and benevolent spirit within us; we are moved to act with compassion and in ways that support those around us. Tolerance and respect afford great protections, as they move us away from judgment—a stance from where we become capable of inflicting harm—and toward acceptance. Each of these states contains its own learnings, which deepen with reflection and practice.

Cultivating Peace: Embracing Nonviolence

A natural outgrowth of Augustine's mercy, tolerance, and respect is nonviolence, a concept that is easily misunderstood. Many people associate it with being soft, passive, or submissive. In fact, the philosophy of nonviolence comes from the Sanskrit word *ahimsa,* and is rooted in a deep commitment to do no harm and refrain from violence. It is an active, life-affirming commitment to respect life in all that we do, as Augustine urged. It is a commitment to life-enhancing rather than life-depleting behavior.

Quakers have been committed to nonviolence and peacemaking for years, and to integrate this philosophy into the fabric of their lives they have long employed a simple, yet effective practice known as the "query." Queries are probing questions that, when thoughtfully engaged, can lead us to decisions grounded in integrity of purpose. Two queries from Britain Yearly Meeting's *Quaker Faith and Practice* demonstrate the subtlety and range inherent in the practice of nonviolence.

Are you honest and truthful in all you say and do? Do you maintain strict integrity in business transactions and in your dealings with individuals and organisations? Do you use money and information entrusted to you with discretion and responsibility? . . .

If pressure is brought upon you to lower your standard of integrity, are you prepared to resist it? Our responsibility to God and our neighbour may involve us in taking unpopular stands. Do not let the desire to be sociable, or the fear of seeming peculiar, determine your decisions.

These two queries provide ways we can realign any actions or behaviors that may be inadvertently creating conflict or harm. The questions allow us to review our intentions and determine whether we are remaining respectful of ourselves and others. The true meaning of the word respect comes from the Latin *respectare*, "the willingness to look again" at ourselves, others, and the circumstances. What difficult person or circumstance are you facing at this time? Use the two queries as a practice to gain clarity and insight into these challenges.

Nonviolence is about respecting and supporting others, and it can be understood along a wide continuum. At one end is the individual desire to avoid harming others in body, mind, or spirit; at the other is a lifelong commitment to nonviolent action for peace and justice for all the peoples of the world. To build a culture of peace, we must align ourselves somewhere on this continuum, for nothing destroys the fabric of peace faster than violence in any form. What is your current relationship to nonviolence? Where do you fall on the continuum? What fixed perspectives do you need to release at this time? Is it time for you to "make peace," to literally create more peace in your life?

Shifting Our Relationship to Conflict

Nonviolence does not mean avoiding conflicts. In *The Peace Book,* Louise Diamond writes, "It simply means to move through them in a clean way, without verbal or physical attacks, to find a peaceful and powerful resolution." Her method and guidelines for a "fair fight" are as follows:

1. Each party has a right to dignity and respect.

2. The process will be a win-win effort so that each party gets their basic needs and interests satisfied.

3. The outcome will leave people feeling better about themselves and each other.

Cross-culturally, conflict is often defined as a call or invitation to creative problem-solving. Mark Gerzon, founder of the Mediator's Foundation, helps leaders and their organizations learn skills that are critical for dealing with conflict, solving problems, and collapsing polarized positions. His foundation's goal is to foster personal and global leadership for a peaceful, just, and sustainable future. The Nebraska Mediation Association offers a thirty-hour training program that provides a non-attorney certificate in conflict resolution that is recognized not only in the state of Nebraska, but nationally as well. The processes of mediation and creative problem-solving give us skills that allow us to move forward through conflict in a consensual and nonviolent manner. As such, any conflict ultimately becomes a gift to be thankful for, a welcome opportunity to create greater harmony and ease for ourselves and others.

When we are conflict-avoidant, we lose both our courage and our creativity. We move toward behaviors such as appeasement, apathy, and avoidance, rather than proactively initiating the necessary opening for resolution. When we lose courage, we may choose to placate someone who is exhibiting hostile behavior: turn away or bury the feelings of distress that naturally emerge whenever we witness an injustice or a calamity. Often, if we believe it is not in our power to help or resolve an uncomfortable situation, we remove ourselves, physically or emotionally. Each of these behaviors radically diminishes our opportunity to create more peace in our lives and in the world.

August is a month to practice bringing forward creative solutions to conflictual areas of our lives. It is a time to stay present and respect the conflict, to be a creative force that does not rescue or fix but works to create the space for win-win possibilities to succeed. In doing so, we must pay special attention and be vigilant to any feelings arising within us that we must win no matter what, and to any tendencies to force a willful resolution through imposing a unilateral decision. These feelings and tendencies are at odds with the respect that must underlie such interactions.

Recognize that when we continue to avoid conflict, one of two things will generally happen: the conflict will accelerate until it causes harm, or it will remain unresolved, becoming an ever present irritant that drains our energy and diminishes our enjoyment of life. One of the consequences of remaining conflict-avoidant is summed up in a well-known saying: "The only thing necessary for the triumph of evil is for good men and women to do nothing."

Sometimes it is important to deliberately generate conflict, to oppose a prevailing situation or stance, and this is especially true when we are a witness to injustice or harm. In accepting the role of challenger to the status quo, the guidelines of a fair fight still apply. We must enter the situation prepared to treat those with opposing views with dignity and respect, work toward a resolution that benefits both sides, and actively create space in which all can emerge from the conflict with a sense of betterment.

Engaging in conflict is one of the ways we develop courage, character, and spiritual depth. This is why it is worth shifting our stance toward conflict—we yield richer lives. The more able we become to move toward and resolve conflict, the more august we become. Be grateful for the conflicts you have successfully resolved in years past, and know that there are as yet unseen gifts in the conflicts to come.

❧

The themes surfacing this month carry great power. Respect is the touchstone of an august life. When we extend respect to ourselves and others we naturally gravitate toward nonviolence, a state we can choose to cultivate in body, mind, and spirit and in thought, word, and deed. As we develop our capacity to embody peace in these ways, we become peacemakers, opening and activating the four portals to gratitude in all our interactions.

AUGUST BENEFIT OF GRATITUDE-PRACTICE

Did you know that the practice of gratitude on a daily basis, over time, increases our resilience and our experiences of contentment, peace, and satisfaction? A common experience that mediators and arbitrators report is their increased capacity to remain curious, hold creative tension, and stay open to seeing new alternatives. Most people who choose these careers are committed to restorative justice and to handling conflict in nonviolent, direct, and honest ways. The practice of gratitude over time strengthens our capacity to face conflict and reduce fear. In what conflictual situations have you experienced gratitude?

Reflections

True victory is victory over one's own aggression.

SUN TZU

In contemplative practices of any kind, questions provoke inquiry, reflection, and conscious awareness of what we are learning or what is being revealed to us about our own current inner and outer work.

Notice which of the following questions capture your attention and which are less evocative or interesting to you at this time. Select two or three of the most meaningful questions for you and explore them more deeply.

- Take time to review your acts of courage in the past decade. What specific feedback have you received from others that you are or have been a source of inspiration? Who or what has been a source of inspiration for you in the last five years?

- Reflect on the most important question from the Talmud: "Have you dealt honorably, faithfully in all your dealings with your fellow-man?" Also reflect on Zusia's question, substituting your own name: "(Your name), why weren't you (your name)?" Where in your life are you not being yourself and why?

- Where have you practiced nonviolence in your life? Our acts of courage often reveal to us our sense of justice or integrity—the urge to do the right thing, even when others may not do the same. It is our courage and integrity that dispel our conflict-avoidant or appeasing patterns. Where we are weak-hearted is where we have courage and integrity work to do. What circumstances or people are calling for your courage at this time?

- Our need to be right or to win gets in the way of resolving conflict in our lives. St. Augustine reminds us of the importance of correcting our own errors. If we own our humanity and correct our mistakes, we reduce our ill will and willfulness. If we do not, we misuse our will. St. Augustine warns us of the consequences of not course-correcting our misuse of will: "It is human to err, but it is devilish to remain willfully in error." Where are you extending ill will or willfulness in your life? Notice and choose to course-correct where this may be happening daily in your relationships.

- Notice the areas of your life where you are consistently extending good will. What fosters your good will?

- Review the qualities that St. Augustine emphasized in his teachings:

humility
mercy
tolerance
respect

Which of these have you experienced or learned from this month? What circumstances evoked your awareness of these qualities and their presence or lack of presence in your life?

Practices

Practices are essential for integrating what we are learning. Select two or three of the following practices that most specifically apply to your current experience and would help you the most at this time.

- For the month of August, practice using Louise Diamond's three guidelines for fair fighting. Practice them in an active conflict, or one you have been avoiding. Notice which of the guidelines are the most challenging and which are the least difficult for you at this time.

- Work with the two Quaker queries for one week as a practice to reduce conflict in your life and maintain your integrity

- Communication and conflict resolution are skills that anyone can learn and practice. Many lifelong learning programs have effective communication classes and conflict-resolution courses. Look for what is available to you in your community. With six to eight weeks of daily practice, anyone can "skill up" in these important areas of life.

- Form a creative-problem-solving group. Share your "best practices": what you have found that works in multiple or diverse circumstances. Highly productive teams use more acknowledgment, have more fun, and are more receptive to each other's ideas. Who would you like to ask to join you in such a group?

- Take an action every day to face areas or circumstances in which you are chronically weak-hearted, or lacking the courage to say what is true for you. Choose to approach the situation with greater strength.

- Make time every day to do something that increases a sense of peace for you, in your internal world as well as your external world.

Review and Integration

Gratitude in the Four Quadrants of Life

work

relationships

**SPIRITUAL GROWTH &
DEVELOPING CHARACTER**

finances

health

Notice what you are grateful for in the four quadrants of your life:

- Work/creative service

- Relationships: friends, colleagues, and family

- Finances and right livelihood

- Health and well-being

The center of the four quadrants represents the place of *developing character* and connecting to your own *spiritual growth* and development. The center is influenced, impacted, and informed by all four quadrants. To help you discover the sources of your gratitude, answer the following tracking questions and see which quadrant or quadrants are emphasized more for you this month.

In looking at the illustration of the Four Quadrants of Life, consider the following questions:

- What are you seeing that is similar to last month's work? What is different, or significantly changing? Review the four quadrants of your life. What is being most activated in either your work, relationships, finances, or health?

- What internal insights and discoveries are you making that have strengthened your character and fostered spiritual growth this month?

- What are you noticing that is new, expanded, or being released in each quadrant of your life this month?

- What are you grateful for in each of your life's quadrants, and how are you expressing your thankfulness?

Blessings, Learnings, Mercies, and Protections

blessings

mercies   *protections*

learnings

Express your gratitude by reflecting upon:

- The major *Blessings* you have given and received during August.

- The major *Learnings* you have given and received during August.

- The major *Mercies* you have given and received during August.

- The major *Protections* you have given and received during August.

The following questions can help you go deeper in your exploration of these four portals to gratitude.

External Questions

- Who or what has inspired you?

- Who or what is challenging you?

- Who or what is surprising you?

- Who or what is touching or moving you?

Internal Questions

- What is strengthening within my nature?

- What is softening within my nature?

- What is opening within my nature?

- What is deepening within my nature?

{ September }

September Prayer

Serenity Prayer

God grant me the SERENITY to
accept the things I cannot change;
COURAGE to change the things I can;
and WISDOM to know the difference.
Living one day at a time;
enjoying one moment at a time;
accepting hardships as the pathway to peace;
taking, as He did, this sinful world
as it is, not as I would have it:
Trusting that He will make all things
right if I surrender to His Will;
that I may be reasonably happy in this life
and supremely happy with Him forever in the next.
Amen.

REINHOLD NIEBUHR (1892–1971)

Opening to
Guidance and
Wisdom

Success is not the key to happiness.
Happiness is the key to success.
If you love what you are doing,
you will be successful.

ALBERT SCHWEITZER

SEPTEMBER ANNOUNCES THE end of summer and the coming of autumn. At the cusp between the two seasons, we experience yet another time of change. Warm, sunny days are interspersed with the first cold, crisp winds of autumn. Flowers might continue to bloom while leaves begin to turn shades of yellow and scarlet. This is a time when many of us return from the faraway places and adventures of summer vacation to resume our work or school lives. In the United States, Labor Day coincides with this homecoming and marks the symbolic end of summer.

In ancient Ireland and Scotland, the word *sept* referred to a clan or sub-clan—or a time when clan or sub-clan members would gather together. When we reunite with friends and colleagues upon return from our summer travels, we echo this ancient ritual and bring with us the renewed perspective that travel affords. In September, we reenter our daily lives from a renewed place and move forward into full engagement. We are able to see more clearly our blessings and our learnings, and we experience the gratitude that naturally results. And we seek opportunities to bring our lives into congruence with the new perspectives we have gained.

In Latin *septem* means "seven" and refers to the seventh month of the year in the pre-Julian calendar. The Judaic holiday, of Rosh Hashanah, which marks the Jewish new year, often occurs in September. This celebration takes place in the seventh month of the Hebrew calendar and offers another opportunity to begin anew.

Opening to Guidance and Wisdom

As we leave the expansiveness of summer and settle into autumn's rhythms and routines, we may discover a desire or longing to integrate our fresh insights. One way to do this is by investigating how others have integrated their own experiences—to open ourselves to systems they have discovered that provided guidance for them. All the spiritual traditions of the world acknowledge that wisdom comes from the accrued learnings of our experiences, and this includes those learnings we reap by following someone else's inspired path for a time. Doing so affords a variety of ways to discover what works and does not work for us on our own unique path.

Roger Walsh, MD, PhD, found that the world religions share seven similar practices to awaken the heart and mind and increase receptivity to inner guidance and wisdom. In his book *Essential Spirituality*, he describes these practices as a universal spiritual map:

- Transform your motivation: reduce craving and find your soul's desire.

- Cultivate emotional wisdom: heal your heart and learn to love.

- Live ethically: feel good by doing good.

- Concentrate and calm your mind.

- Awaken your spiritual vision: see clearly and recognize the sacred in all things.

- Cultivate spiritual intelligence: develop wisdom and understand life.

- Express spirit in action: embrace generosity and the joy of service.

When we look at the first three of the seven universal practices, we can see natural benefits that are available to us to increase our well-being. For example, when we love what we do and find it satisfying and meaningful, we have stepped into our soul's desire, purpose, or calling and we stop striving, craving, or chasing unrealistic expectations of ourselves and others. When we heal our hearts, we no longer blame others or hold onto past grudges, resentments, or disappointments. Releasing the past enables us to reach out and help others by doing good works, such as offering aid to someone who is ill or struggling financially; when we do so, we feel good, for we know that it is the ethical and right thing to do. Each of these seven universal practices contains similar benefits that nourish the spirit.

Within each practice, the world's religions include exercises to cultivate kindness, love, joy, peace, vision, wisdom, and generosity. The development of these qualities not only fosters our well-being but generates increased blessings and natural abundance in our lives. As we develop new positive habits internally, we can reassess our external effectiveness and open to new guidance and fresh possibilities. Notice which of these practices you may already be engaged in, and which you are not.

In his book *The Seven Habits of Highly Effective People,* Stephen Covey defines a positive habit as the intersection of knowledge, skill, and desire. He has identified seven habits that are consistently used by highly effective people, and has developed a program to help others become equally effective in their personal and professional lives. The seven habits are:

1. Be proactive (take initiative).

2. Begin with the end in mind.

3. Put first things first.

4. Think win-win.

5. Seek to understand, rather than be understood.

6. Synergize (create something larger than the sum of its parts).

7. Sharpen the saw (commit to regular times of self-renewal).

Covey is convinced that these behaviors help us achieve a sense of unity—oneness with ourselves, loved ones, friends, and associates. When we experience such unity, we benefit from the best of the seven habits. Consistently applied, the habits foster congruence and clear focus that can be applied to whatever is at the center of our lives—whether it is work, relationships, health, finances, community, church, or adventure. He writes, "Whatever is at the center of our life will be the source of our security, guidance, wisdom, and power. . . . Security and clear guidance bring true wisdom, and wisdom becomes the spark or catalyst to release and direct power. When these four factors are present together, harmonized and enlivened by each other, they create the great force of a noble personality, a balanced character, a beautifully integrated individual."

Which of these habits is most developed and which is least developed for you at this time? Where do you stand?

What is at the center of your life at this time? What is your central motivation now? Often our central motivation, if acted upon, increases our sense of self and security. Whenever we have the experience of being ourselves, or of loving what we are doing, we arrive at the center of what is important for us. In using Covey's habits consistently in the areas of our life where we are centrally motivated, we increase our capacities for self-confidence, trust, developing wisdom, and opening to guidance, and this promotes our own well-being and that of others. What guidance or wisdom are you opening to now that is strengthening your nature or motivating you to become a more effective individual?

In September, by opening ourselves to both our internal guidance and the wisdom of others, we have the opportunity to choose practices that will help us develop our best qualities. We can draw from Walsh or Covey or from another who presents us with the gift of a tried-and-true system to explore.

The Role of the Body

To achieve positive change, we must also attend to maintaining our physical health. The body has its own wisdom. Many of us are familiar with the old saying, "Pay attention to what your body is telling you. It does not lie." In his book *The Power of Infinite Love and Gratitude,* Dr. Darren R. Weissman has found that if we attend to the five basics of optimum health, we access more easily the power of infinite love and gratitude. This involves attending to the "quantity, quality, and frequency of *drinking water, eating, resting, exercising,* and *owning our own power.*" He is convinced that attending to these five areas of health will allow us not only to sustain our health but to achieve optimal health.

We have all been told about the importance of the first four basic body needs, yet we seldom attend to them consistently with the quality, quantity, and frequency that are needed. The last basic principle of health he mentions, owning one's power, is an equally essential component of maintaining health. Weissman and many other researchers and health professionals have documented that not attending to our self-esteem, chronically feeling disempowered, mistrusting ourselves, or giving our power away in relationships can all reduce our health, stamina, vitality, and mental and emotional well-being. Furthermore, in his book *Deep Medicine,* Dr. William Stewart, director of the Institute for Health and Healing at the California Pacific Medical Center in San Francisco, demonstrates how health increases or decreases according to the choices we make. He stresses how important it is to monitor our choices, and offers the most important question for us to ask ourselves when we are making a decision: "Is this a health-enhancing choice, or a health-negating choice?"

What are the quality, quantity, and frequency of your intake of water and food? What balance are you maintaining between rest and exercise? Where do you own your power throughout the day, and to what and whom do you give it away? How do you integrate your healthy choices with your efforts to increase your external and internal effectiveness?

It has been well documented that the daily practice of gratitude increases health and well-being. Genuine expression of gratitude reduces stress, develops positive attitudes and performance, strengthens the immune system, and increases our experience of joy and happiness. Mike Robbins, a sports coach and author of *Focus on the Good Stuff: The Power of Appreciation,* offers five principles of appreciation, which are: "be grateful; choose positive thoughts and feelings; use positive words; acknowledge others; appreciate yourself." He has found that when appreciation is expressed genuinely, spontaneously—and often—performance, self-confidence, and well-being all increase. What increases in your own health and well-being have you noticed as a result of your practice of living in gratitude?

In September, as summer fades and we turn to embrace autumn's great bounty and gifts, we enjoy a renewed perspective of the seasons of life. We are motivated to make time to identify and explore what lies at our life's center, and our resulting awareness brings opportunities to investigate new pathways to a better life. Opening to guidance and wisdom in a variety of ways affords us greater access to the infinite power of love and gratitude.

SEPTEMBER BENEFIT OF GRATITUDE-PRACTICE

John Demartini discovered that the more people count their blessings and give gratitude, the more their health and sense of well-being increase. He developed the Demartini Method, derived from quantum physics, which neutralizes emotional charges and brings balance to both mind and body. The process involves a predetermined set of questions and actions surrounding gratitude and blessings that allows us to break through to new levels of inspiration, creativity, performance, and health. Spend this month counting your blessings and offering gratitude for them. Notice the benefits you derive as a result, and how opening to guidance and wisdom fosters even more appreciation.

Reflections

The human spirit is too large to accept a cage for its home.

Huston Smith

In contemplative practices of any kind, questions provoke inquiry, reflection, and conscious awareness of what we are learning or what is being revealed to us about our own current inner and outer work.

Notice which of the following questions capture your attention and which are less evocative or interesting to you at this time. Select two or three of the most meaningful questions for you and explore them more deeply.

- In what areas of your life do you trust your own guidance and wisdom? In what ways are you opening to the guidance and wisdom of others?

- Which of the seven spiritual practices on Roger Walsh's list have you most developed? Which have you least developed? To strengthen your internal work, choose one or two of these to reflect upon this month.

- Appreciate what is working in your life. See which of Stephen Covey's seven habits of highly effective people you are applying now. Which ones are challenging for you?

- At the end of each day, acknowledge to yourself the excellent work and creativity you have extended to your family and coworkers. Notice where you have genuinely acknowledged the particular gifts, talents, skills, and character qualities you have observed in others. Whatever and whomever we appreciate, including ourselves, appreciates (increases in value), amplifies, or expands.

- Notice what motivates your expression of gratitude and appreciation this month.

- Health and longevity studies show that when people live with a sense of purpose, no matter how big or small, they live longer and healthier lives. What sense of purpose or central focus consistently motivates you?

- In maintaining health and well-being in all aspects of our life, it is important to track the choices we are making. As Dr. William Stewart suggests, ask yourself, "Is this a health enhancing choice, or a health negating choice?" Will this choice enrich or undermine my health, finances, relationships, work, or character? Review the decisions you are making this month. Are they life enhancing or life negating?

Practices

Practices are essential for integrating what we are learning. Select two or three of the following practices that most specifically apply to your current experience and would help you the most at this time.

- Commit to memory the "Serenity Prayer" or read it before counting your blessings for the day. Give gratitude for your blessings.

- For the next six weeks, practice giving quality, quantity, and frequent time and attention to the five principles that support optimum health according to Dr. Darren Weissman: water, food, rest, exercise, and owning your power.

- Listen to your body wisdom and take action on whatever it needs. Create a support system that helps you stay focused on the five principles that sustain and maintain optimal health.

- Which of the spiritual practices identified by Roger Walsh are the most developed for you at this time? Choose at least three that you would like to strengthen this month and take action to do so.

- Of Stephen Covey's seven habits, this month strengthen the ones that you currently practice the least.

- Practice Mike Robbins's five principles of appreciation for two weeks. Notice the changes in your performance, self-confidence, and well-being.

- Create a bulletin board of blessings for the month, or use any other visual aid, so you can *see* as well as *count* your blessings.

- Practice increasing your life-enhancing choices on a daily basis this month.

Review and Integration

Gratitude in the Four Quadrants of Life

work

relationships

**SPIRITUAL GROWTH &
DEVELOPING CHARACTER**

finances

health

Notice what you are grateful for in the four quadrants of your life:

- Work/creative service

- Relationships: friends, colleagues, and family

- Finances and right livelihood

- Health and well-being

The center of the four quadrants represents the place of *developing character* and connecting to your own *spiritual growth* and development. The center is influenced, impacted, and informed by all four quadrants. To help you discover the sources of your gratitude, answer the following tracking questions and see which quadrant or quadrants are emphasized more for you this month.

In looking at the illustration of the Four Quadrants of Life, consider the following questions:

- What are you seeing that is similar to last month's work? What is different, or significantly changing? Review the four quadrants of your life. What is being most activated in either your work, relationships, finances, or health?

- What internal insights and discoveries are you making that have strengthened your character and fostered spiritual growth this month?

- What are you noticing that is new, expanded, or being released in each quadrant of your life this month?

- What are you grateful for in each of your life's quadrants, and how are you expressing your thankfulness?

Blessings, Learnings, Mercies, and Protections

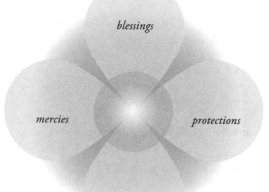

Express your gratitude by reflecting upon:

- The major *Blessings* you have given and received during September

- The major *Learnings* you have given and received during September

- The major *Mercies* you have given and received during September

- The major *Protections* you have given and received during September

The following questions can help you go deeper in your exploration of these four portals to gratitude.

External Questions

- Who or what has inspired you?

- Who or what is challenging you?

- Who or what is surprising you?

- Who or what is touching or moving you?

Internal Questions

- What is strengthening within my nature?

- What is softening within my nature?

- What is opening within my nature?

- What is deepening within my nature?

{ October }

October Prayer

Prayer of Thanks

For each new morning with its light,

for rest and shelter of the night,

For health and food,

For love and friends,

For everything Thy goodness sends,

Father in heaven,

We thank thee.

RALPH WALDO EMERSON (1803–1882)

Letting Be
and Letting Go

A hundred times every day I remind myself
that my inner and outer life
depend on the labours of other men,
living and dead, and that I must exert myself
in order to give in the same measure
as I have received and am still receiving.

ALBERT EINSTEIN

OCTOBER SIGNALS THE midpoint of autumn. Deciduous trees have reached the height of their fall colors, the air is crisp and invigorating, and we now prepare to harvest what we have set in motion earlier in the year.

On the last day of the month the people of the United States and Latin America respectively celebrate Halloween and All Saints' Day, or All Souls' Day, the commemoration of the faithful departed. In contemporary times, our Halloween ritual is marked by masquerading. We dress our children in costumes and walk from door to door saying, "Trick or treat!" Give us a treat or we'll trick you! Or we celebrate by gathering at costume parties, delighting in one another's clever and outrageous getups. In many places in Europe, large puppets mingle with the crowds in All Saints' celebrations held in the streets.

Originally, Halloween, *to make hallow or holy,* was an evening to venerate the unseen world and honor the souls who have gone before us. While we have largely left this custom behind, it lives on in the images of skeletons and ghosts found everywhere at this time.

In ancient Europe, harvest festivals—known, for example, as Oktoberfest in Germany—were held, a tradition that has endured to this day. These are occasions when we come together to literally enjoy the fruits of our labors in the fields, orchards, and pastures. It is a time of great bounty when we share with others what we have produced: an annual celebration of gratitude. If, in our contemporary life, we are not directly connected to the land and its abundant gifts in such a way, we still have the opportunity to appreciate the season's offerings of apples, pears, pumpkins, and other fall crops. Giving gratitude for these nourishing foods can be our own personal Oktoberfest.

Letting Be and Letting Go

George Bernard Shaw best described what we may experience during October when he wrote, "A day's work is a day's work, neither more nor less, and the man who does it needs a day's sustenance, a night's repose and due leisure, whether he be painter or plowman." Our labors leading to the harvest are important, but equally so is leaving the fields and other work in order to nourish the body and spirit.

Letting be and *letting go* are two processes that challenge us every day to accept things as they are, especially during times of change. The state of letting be requires us to increase our levels of trust and acceptance of what is occurring in the moment, without pushing or holding back to attempt to create a different experience. Letting go is a willingness to release, in the moment, what might impede our progress. When we sense resistance in letting go, this may be a signal where we are overly attached or controlling. During times of harvest, nature reminds and challenges us to notice our capacities for letting be and letting go.

These two practices are inherent to the human species and are the counterpoint to our striving. Every culture recognizes that developing certain life skills is necessary in order to navigate change.

Theologian Matthew Fox says that as a species, we have much to learn about the deeper lessons of living and being human. Among these he cites four important ones:

- The dark night as a learning place

- The softening and watering of the heart

- The awakening of imagination, play, and the creative impulse nourishes the quest for repose

- The purification of our longing—What do we truly cherish, truly long for? What sacrifices are we willing to undergo to obtain that which we long for?

All four of these deeper lessons of life require us to let be and let go. Facing what we learn in the dark night compels us to let go of self-deception or illusion, to let be and accept where we are now—and where we are not. Awakening to what nurtures us means letting go of what does not nurture us, and letting be what does. Our longings, when purified by clarity, allow us to align with what is meaningful and provides fulfilling growth. Achieving clarity requires the intentional sacrifices of letting go of what is not in alignment with our longing.

The true meaning of sacrifice comes from the root word *sacra:* to make sacred. Once we are clear about what is important in what we long for, we can recognize the issues and obstacles that are in the way. It is in this recognition that we become committed to sacrificing or releasing the obstructions that impede the actualization of our longing. These conscious sacrifices simultaneously purify our longings and provide a means for them to manifest.

These lessons of living and being human—of harvest, of letting be, and of letting go—surface in the fall as we prepare for winter and the close of the year. From the fruits, or *treats,* of our labors, we get to see that what we have best attended to has manifested because it has truly mattered to us. What did not come to fruition, or what did not hold our interest, may reveal where we *tricked* ourselves, and it shows us that it did not truly matter. We learn that what has heart and meaning for us comes into being, and that in contrast, any ambivalence or doubt we may feel often produces inconsistent results—or none at all. Consider what you are harvesting now in this light.

Whatever we have accepted both internally and externally, we can let be. And it is often the case that when we can let be, we can let go. For example, if we unexpectedly lose work that we love, yet we are convinced that we can find something else effortlessly, it is easier to let go and let be. Externally, we have lost a job. Internally, we have the confidence that we can find something new effortlessly. We can let go of the old ways and let the situation be, with faith that new opportunities are at hand. If, on the other hand, we are attached to the outer form of our work, and internally we do not believe it can be replaced, it is much more difficult to let go and let be. What circumstances allow you to attend to the deeper lessons of living and being human that Matthew Fox has identified? What are you letting be, and what are you letting go of in your work, relationships, health, or within yourself at this time?

Involvement in Community

Harvests and celebrations involve bringing clusters of people together and are essentially community endeavors. The word *community* (common-unity) comes from two Latin words that mean "fellowship" and "shared by all." Community is natural to our species, as it is to the rest of nature. The season of fall insists that we balance the harvest of individual contributions with those of the community as a whole.

Human beings are happiest in groups where they can share or contribute the most, whether they are participating in the joys of life or its tragedies. Longing and belonging may be opposites, but both are satisfied by community, which fosters togetherness and offers a place to fulfill our desires. This is a good time to consider the communities of which you are a part: your family and extended family; your workplace; a church, temple, or meditation circle; a social or environmental cause; your neighborhood or city. The communities to which we belong reveal what matters to us. How many groups or communities do you serve or celebrate? What are you moved to contribute to each of them in this season of harvest?

We are the ancestors of tomorrow's communities. We are preparing the way for new generations. We have a moral responsibility to pass on to those not yet born a world of beauty and health. What do you see, hope for, and want to create that would benefit generations of the future? Every grandparent, for example, longs for their grandchildren to have greater access to healthy natural environments, a better education, and more opportunities to manifest what they love—and to have the means with which to do so. What will you contribute today that will be relevant and necessary for those yet to come?

Peter Block, author of *The Answer to How Is Yes,* invites us to become social architects in our lives, which means committing and engaging with others to manifest what matters most. Block defines social architecture as "an image, a role for each of us to create . . . it gives some guidance as to how we might bring our willingness to act on values, on what matters, into the collective and institutional arena . . . it recognizes that acting on what matters for one person will happen in concert with those around that person. Individual effort will not be enough."

A social architect provides space to explore what is truly important while addressing the deeper lessons of living and being human within the community. When we follow what is most essential to us and support what matters most to others, we create openings where each individual's gifts and talents can be used and honored. We have all had the experience of being a social architect whenever we have worked within any team effort: a theatre ensemble, a sports team, a social movement, or a choir. When everyone's gifts are valued, aligned, and expressed in what they love, the results are always greater than any one individual could achieve. What matters most to you at this time? In what ways are you functioning as a social architect in your life? When we assume this role in any community endeavor, we align our actions in accordance with our values and we respect and appreciate the contributions of others.

Harvesting What Matters

Take time this month to practice appreciation and genuine acknowledgment of the gifts that surround you. This is a practice that involves all the themes of the month—celebrating, letting be, letting go, longing, and belonging to community—as we begin to harvest those things we have been willing to commit to. Real commitment is a choice we make regardless of what is offered in return. Notice the unexpected opportunities or results that have come to fruition because you have been fully committed to a project or an important relationship. Often, when we are committed to what has heart and meaning, our work is so satisfying in itself that we manifest a level of excellence that others recognize. The motive for actors, for example, is to play a part well; seldom is it to get an Academy Award. When an actor's work is recognized, it is a reflection of his or her personal commitment.

❧

The month of October is inherently beautiful. Trees are aflame with color, crops are ripe and bountiful, and we come together for joyful community celebrations. Such external beauty mirrors our internal richness as we harvest the fruits of our inner work. This allows us to let be and let go, reminding us to be with things as they are. Offer thanks to yourself for your efforts and insights at this time. Acknowledge your communities for the blessings, learnings, mercies, and protections they afford, and for your opportunities to contribute to them. The month of the harvest is an important milestone on our journey to living in gratitude.

OCTOBER BENEFIT OF GRATITUDE-PRACTICE

One thing every social architect has in common is a deep commitment to learning and fostering the gifts and talents of others as well as their own. Dr. William Glasser has spent many years studying how people learn, and has expanded Edgar Dale's educational percentages and theories on how we learn:

Edgar Dale's Educational Percentages and Theories on How We Learn

- 10% of what we read
- 20% of what we hear
- 30% of what we see
- 50% of what we see *and* hear

- 70% of what we discuss with others
- 80% of what we experience personally
- 95% of what we teach to someone else

Practicing what we learn and relating it to others is part of being a social architect, and the give and take involved requires the ability to let go and let be. Learning communities help us integrate our experience and express our own learnings on a deeper level. Our learning increases exponentially when we discuss what is meaningful for us with others, when we experience something personally that is invaluable, or when we teach what we have learned to someone else. In any learning environment that increases our own personal value, creativity, and productivity, our expression of gratitude for other people's gifts and talents increases as well. Every social architect, in order to be effective, has to have the ability to let go and let be.

Reflections

To transform itself in us, the future enters into us long before it happens.

RAINER MARIA RILKE

In contemplative practices of any kind, questions provoke inquiry, reflection, and conscious awareness of what we are learning or what is being revealed to us about our own current inner and outer work.

Notice which of the following questions capture your attention and which are less evocative or interesting to you at this time. Select two or three of the most meaningful questions for you and explore them more deeply.

- At this time in your life, what are you letting go of; what are you allowing to let be; what are you harvesting?

- How has October revealed the *treats* or fruits of your labors this year? What have been the *tricks* or surprises of this year? What have you learned this month?

- Since October is seen as the month of many fests or festivals, what has awakened in your imagination, what is fun for you—and in contrast, what prompts you to seek time alone for reflection?

- What do you find yourself longing for at this time? What interest groups or communities are you participating in as a visible member?

- Peter Block reminds us that a social architect fosters individual and collective opportunities in a space where others can also act on what matters to them. In what areas of your life are you functioning as a social architect?

- In what ways are you contributing to make the world a better place for the generations of the future?

Practices

Practices are essential for integrating what we are learning. Select two or three of the following practices that most specifically apply to your current experience and would help you the most at this time.

- What really matters to you at this time? Are you creating a life that matters? What specific actions will you take this month to support what truly matters to you?

- Where we surrender and accept things as they are, we can let be and let go. This month, practice letting be (a practice of increasing trust and acceptance of what is) and letting go (a practice of releasing attachment and control) in those areas that are most challenging for you to do so.

- Collect colorful fall leaves. On yellow ones, write your learnings this month; use red ones for heartfelt gratitudes. Use white paper on which to write down your longings, and then purify your longings by burning the paper in fire. Do the same thing for any regrets you may have experienced this year. How can you rectify these issues after you have burned them, or choose to do things differently next time?

- The interest groups we form are ways we create community. What new groups do you belong to and what gifts and talents are you offering to these groups? This month, practice creating openings where your own gifts and talents can supplement or enhance the gifts and talents of others.

- This month, increase your learning by noticing what you are discussing with others; your learning increases 70 percent by doing this. What are you personally experiencing that is deeply meaningful for you? Personal experience helps you retain 80 percent of your learning. What are you teaching others or helping others learn? Ninety-five percent of this learning will be absorbed. What has strengthened in your learning this month? Practice accelerating your learning in conversations with others, or teach what you love to those who might be interested in learning.

- Find ways to express your gratitude for what you have harvested this month, and what has come to fruition this year. Put it into words aloud, in a poem or journal entry, or in a silent prayer of thanks.

Review and Integration

Gratitude in the Four Quadrants of Life

Notice what you are grateful for in the four quadrants of your life:

- Work/creative service

- Relationships: friends, colleagues, and family

- Finances and right livelihood

- Health and well-being

The center of the four quadrants represents the place of *developing character* and connecting to your own *spiritual growth* and development. The center is influenced, impacted, and informed by all four quadrants. To help you discover the sources of your gratitude, answer the following tracking questions and see which quadrant or quadrants are emphasized more for you this month.

In looking at the illustration of the Four Quadrants of Life, consider the following questions:

- What are you seeing that is similar to last month's work? What is different, or significantly changing? Review the four quadrants of your life. What is being most activated in either your work, relationships, finances, or health?

- What internal insights and discoveries are you making that have strengthened your character and fostered spiritual growth this month?

- What are you noticing that is new, expanded, or being released in each quadrant of your life this month?

- What are you grateful for in each of your life's quadrants, and how are you expressing your thankfulness?

Blessings, Learnings, Mercies, and Protections

blessings

mercies   protections

learnings

Express your gratitude by reflecting upon:

- The major *Blessings* you have given and received during October.

- The major *Learnings* you have given and received during October.

- The major *Mercies* you have given and received during October.

- The major *Protections* you have given and received during October.

The following questions can help you go deeper in your exploration of these four portals to gratitude.

External Questions

- Who or what has inspired you?

- Who or what is challenging you?

- Who or what is surprising you?

- Who or what is touching or moving you?

Internal Questions

- What is strengthening within my nature?

- What is softening within my nature?

- What is opening within my nature?

- What is deepening within my nature?

{ November }

November Prayer

Thanksgiving Prayer of the
Haudenosaunee Nation

We return thanks to our mother, the earth,
Which sustains us.
We return thanks to the rivers and streams,
Which supply us with water.
We return thanks to all herbs,
Which furnish medicines for the cure of our diseases.
We return thanks to the moon and the stars,
Which have given us their light
When the sun was gone.
We return thanks to the sun,
That has looked upon the earth with a beneficent eye.
Lastly, we return thanks to the Great Spirit,
In Whom is embodied all goodness,
And Who directs all things
for the good of Her children.

ADAPTED FROM FIRST NATION'S PRAYER

Grateful Seeing

*List your blessings and you will walk through
those gates of thanksgiving and into the fields of joy.*

GARRISON KEILLOR

IN NOVEMBER WE continue to honor the beauty and
bounty of autumn. Americans long ago dedicated a day
during this month for the sole purpose of inviting and expressing gratitude. We know this day by its traditional name,
Thanksgiving. For those of us consciously choosing to live in
gratitude, this month presents a unique opportunity to not
only deepen our own experience of thankfulness, but to share
it explicitly with those around us. What a gift it is that we
are annually invited—even urged—to answer the simple yet
powerful question, "What are you thankful for today?"

Though Thanksgiving itself is but a single day, gratitude occupies our thoughts frequently this month as we
anticipate the arrival of the holiday. Family members make

arrangements to travel. Cooks plan menus, shop, and prepare to receive guests. These are some of the rituals of our modern Thanksgiving, and they offer frequent reminders of the reason we are celebrating: because our lives are bountiful. If we are blessed with plenty at this time, our holiday may take the form of a large gathering and a generous feast. If our means are more modest, the day may involve a simple meal with a friend after a long nature walk. Or we may choose to spend an afternoon at a community center feeding those who have little. The holiday is what we make of it, but it always holds the promise of renewed awareness of all our blessings, large and small.

Reflecting on Fruition

Thanksgiving is a time to harvest, appreciate, and celebrate those things that have come to fruition in our lives during the year, in both external and internal ways. Perhaps a valued relationship has deepened. We may have seen a project through from idea to reality, become confident in a new skill, or noticed that we have integrated an important experience that has made us wiser. As we answer the question "What are you thankful for today?" it is important to appreciate the work we have done to bring us to this point in our journey. This is a time to celebrate our sustained intention and efforts, for they have borne fruit.

When Mother Teresa was asked about the fruit of her work, she often responded by listing the six fruits of life she was most grateful for:

The fruit of silence is prayer,
The fruit of prayer is faith,
The fruit of faith is love,
The fruit of love is service,
The fruit of service is peace.

The internal fruits of silence and prayer cultivated and strengthened Mother Teresa's love and faith and provided her the courage to extend these qualities to the dying poor in India. Her external efforts were recognized when she received the Nobel Peace Prize for her work and, after her death, was beatified by the Catholic Church.

Like Mother Teresa, others such as Gandhi, Golda Meir, and Martin Luther King, Jr. were moved by the internal fruits of faith, prayer, and compassion to manifest the external fruits of their work in the world and their place in history. What internal fruits are motivating the external work that you love in the world at this time?

The role of silence in the progression Mother Teresa spoke of cannot be underestimated—there is great power in it. When we spend time in silence and deeply listen to the guidance given, our actions in the outer world align with what has heart and meaning for us.

Cross-Cultural Traditions

Every culture of the world has its own harvest rituals and ways of sharing its bounty, as well as releasing what is not needed or giving it away. Our Thanksgiving tradition, for example, is rooted in the story of how Native Americans helped the Pilgrims survive and taught them to give thanks for Earth's abundance. Many traditional peoples of this continent have considered fall the best season for extending generosity of spirit, and they have done so by giving gratitude and thanksgiving for the abundance in their lives. Some have done this through the practice of "the give-away": offering to others things that are deeply valued, or giving away that which is not being used to those who are in greater need.

In some native cultures of the Pacific Northwest, the giveaway takes the form of the potlatch, a celebration during which tangible things such as food and decorative items are offered, as are intangible gifts such as songs or dances. These acts are ways of expressing and cultivating generosity of spirit. Island peoples of the world have daily rituals, songs of praise, and prayers for giving thanks for the bounty received from the sea, for food provided by the land, and for each other.

November is the month of letting go of what is no longer needed or has fulfilled its purpose, just as trees now release the last season's leaves. In China, an old proverb speaks to this: "Give away, throw away or move twenty-seven items for nine days and your life will change!" The practice of letting go teaches us about nonattachment. The process of releasing or emptying provides room for new possibilities, opportunities, and blessings to enter our lives.

The Mirror of the Breath

The harvesting and releasing rituals practiced by world cultures are mirrored in each of us through the breath. Breathing is a practice in releasing, opening, and receiving the blessing of life. In his book *Forgive for Good*, Fred Luskin offers the Breath of Thanks exercise, which we can do on a daily basis as a gratitude and letting-go practice:

1. Two or three times every day when you are not fully occupied, slow down and bring your attention to your breathing.

2. Notice how your breath flows in and out without your having to do anything. . . .

3. Continue breathing this way for about three to five slow, deep breaths.

4. For each of the next five to eight inhalations, say the words *thank you* silently to remind yourself of the gift of your breath and how lucky you are to be alive.

Luskin suggests practicing this exercise at least three times a week; it is a good reminder that gratitude begins with the basics. Embodying gratitude in this way is a practice that is available to us all, regardless of our current circumstances. At Thanksgiving time, it is important to give thanks for the great gift of life itself that is carried along by the breath. We can also appreciate the breath as a unifying force; each time we inhale and exhale, we share a universal experience and are thereby joined with the rest of humanity and with all the other species of the world.

A Shift in Perspective: Grateful Seeing

In November we can readily see how much we have to be thankful for compared to our troubles and dissatisfactions. As we extend gratitude for the bounty and goodness that are present in our lives, any pockets of ingratitude that once seemed large in our imaginations become dwarfed—nearly nonexistent. It is important to remember that whatever we need to rectify in our lives is often small in proportion to all the benefits we have extended toward and received from others. All the good intentions, prayers, good deeds, and kind words we have offered others are still with us: they cannot be taken away, and this is a great source of encouragement.

Emmet Fox, a scientist, philosopher, and spiritual teacher, reminds us that "Errors of thought, word, and deed are worked out and satisfied under the Law, but the good goes on forever, unchanged and undimmed by time." Dacher Keltner, a researcher at the University of California, Berkeley, and author of *Born to Be Good: The Science of a Meaningful Life,* demonstrates that the intrinsic value that lies within the human spirit is not only to be a good human being, but to foster more goodness and well-being for others in meaningful ways. His research also indicates that the good that occurs in our lives, whether we have extended it or received it, is far more valued and remembered in our hearts than our errors or mistakes.

November offers us a time to honor and be thankful for all the goodness that life, loved ones, and important strangers have extended to us. What goodness are you known for at this time in your life? Make it a point to see and appreciate the fruits of goodness in your colleagues, your friends, and your family. When we see more fruits than errors, we have developed grateful seeing.

Grateful seeing is the ability to look first for what is good and working in our lives without minimizing or denying the hardships or challenges that are also present. Many traditional societies hold the perspective, or world view, that what has been given to us ultimately ignites growth and strengthens us. Individuals who are viewed as seers in indigenous societies are highly respected, honored, and valued for their gifts of insight, vision, and grateful seeing. The Maasai of East Africa, for example, call their seers *diviners,* ones who perceive in the seen and unseen worlds that which is divine and good. We, too, can learn to be seers—seers of the blessings, learnings, mercies, and protections that are ever present.

Focusing on the benefits and goodness that are all around us leads to feelings of gratitude, and this creates a multiplier effect: the experience of gratitude generates a sense of well-being, and the better we feel, the more good we will do. Gratitude and the actions it stimulates also build and strengthen social bonds and friendships. This practice of grateful seeing, looking for the good, allows us to see the gift of love—given and received—that is present in our lives.

One definition of a miracle is a change in perspective; therefore our focus on grateful seeing in November can make it a month of miracles. Looking for the bounty and good in our lives creates a disposition for gratitude and allows us to see that some of the challenges we face may be blessings in disguise. Look for the areas of your life where your efforts have borne fruit. Be grateful for the works you have created, within and without. Acknowledge the gifts you have received and the thoughts, prayers, and kindnesses you have extended to others. Shift your perspective from looking first to what is not working in your life to looking first at what is. Dedicate this month to giving thanks, and this will strengthen your capacity for grateful seeing.

NOVEMBER BENEFIT OF GRATITUDE-PRACTICE

Did you know that empirical studies show that gratitude engenders behaviors typically endorsed as moral and good? Gratitude increases our inclinations to be more caring, compassionate, just, honest, and respectful towards others. Such behaviors reinforce the inherent sense of goodness within human beings. People who extend or are recipients of these behaviors experience a sense of connection and appreciation for the goodness given and received. When we begin to look for the good in our lives and shift our perspective to see what *is* working, our experience of grateful seeing and our expression of gratitude increase significantly.

Reflections

Yesterday is history. Tomorrow is a mystery. Today is a gift!

ANONYMOUS

In contemplative practices of any kind, questions provoke inquiry, reflection, and conscious awareness of what we are learning or what is being revealed to us about our own current inner and outer work.

Notice which of the following questions capture your attention and which are less evocative or interesting to you at this time. Select two or three of the most meaningful questions for you and explore them more deeply.

- What are you thankful for today?

- In what ways do you express your gratitude? How do others know that you are grateful?

- What family rituals and expressions of gratitude have been passed on to you? Which ones have you continued? What new ones have you originated?

- As the year begins to wind to a close, reflect every day of this month upon the blessings, opportunities, fruits, and harvests that have come into your life this year. To whom or what are you especially grateful for in your life?

- In what ways are you shifting your perspective from looking at what is not working to developing "grateful seeing"—looking first for what is working and what is good in your life?

- Whom have you helped this year? What circumstances have ignited your generosity and gratitude?

- What positive changes have occurred in your life that you can directly attribute to your gratitude practices this year?

Practices

Practices are essential for integrating what we are learning. Select two or three of the following practices that most specifically apply to your current experience and would help you the most at this time.

- Practice generosity of spirit by giving to the needy or offering anonymous acts of kindness. Clear out what you are not using or do not need and give it away to those who could use it. Go back to the month of March and review your choices about compassionate service. How has your compassion increased since then?

- Write letters, call, or send gifts of gratitude to those who have provided blessings in your life.

- Practice looking for the goodness and fruits of generosity and love in your life. As Emmet Fox says, "good goes

on forever, unchanged, and undimmed." Notice what
changes as a result of changing your perspective from
what is not working to what is working.

- Each morning, take a moment to pay attention to your
breath and to give thanks for life (regardless of how your
life feels at the moment). Use Fred Luskin's Breath of
Thanks exercise at least three times a week this month.

- Practice appreciating the gift of each day. Remember the
philosophy of being present to the blessings and learnings
each day offers—"Yesterday is history. Tomorrow is a
mystery. Today is a gift."

- Spend at least fifteen minutes a day in silence and deep
listening. Take time to rebalance, rest, and come back
to your center or ground of being—that grace-filled
sanctuary of quiet, stillness, and peace that Mother
Teresa and others drew from in order to do their good
works in the world.

- Write your own poem, prayer, or story for Thanksgiving.

Review and Integration

Gratitude in the Four Quadrants of Life

work *relationships*

**SPIRITUAL GROWTH &
DEVELOPING CHARACTER**

finances *health*

Notice what you are grateful for in the four quadrants of your life:

- Work/creative service

- Relationships: friends, colleagues, and family

- Finances and right livelihood

- Health and well-being

The center of the four quadrants represents the place of *developing character* and connecting to your own *spiritual growth* and development. The center is influenced, impacted, and informed by all four quadrants. To help you discover the sources of your gratitude, answer the following tracking questions and see which quadrant or quadrants are emphasized more for you this month.

In looking at the illustration of the Four Quadrants of Life, consider the following questions:

- What are you seeing that is similar to last month's work? What is different, or significantly changing? Review the four quadrants of your life. What is being most activated in either your work, relationships, finances, or health?

- What internal insights and discoveries are you making that have strengthened your character and fostered spiritual growth this month?

- What are you noticing that is new, expanded, or being released in each quadrant of your life this month?

- What are you grateful for in each of your life's quadrants, and how are you expressing your thankfulness?

Blessings, Learnings, Mercies, and Protections

Express your gratitude by reflecting upon:

- The major *Blessings* you have given and received during November.

- The major *Learnings* you have given and received during November.

- The major *Mercies* you have given and received during November.

- The major *Protections* you have given and received during November.

The following questions can help you go deeper in your exploration of these four portals to gratitude.

External Questions

- Who or what has inspired you?

- Who or what is challenging you?

- Who or what is surprising you?

- Who or what is touching or moving you?

Internal Questions

- What is strengthening within my nature?

- What is softening within my nature?

- What is opening within my nature?

- What is deepening within my nature?

{ December }

December Prayer

An Islamic Prayer for Peace
*In the Name of Allah,
the beneficent, the merciful:
Praise be to the Lord of the
Universe who has created us and
made us into tribes and nations
that we may know each other,
not that we may despise each other.
If the enemy incline towards peace,
do thou also incline towards peace, and
trust in God, for the Lord is the one that
hears and knows all things.
And the servants of God Most Gracious
are those who walk on
the Earth in humility; and when we
address them, we say, "Peace."*

The Mystic Heart

*The utterances of the heart, unlike those of
the discriminating intellect, always relate to the whole.
In this sense, the heart shows the meaning of things
in great perspective. What the heart hears
are the great things that span our whole lives,
the experiences which we do nothing to arrange
but which simply happen to us.*

CARL JUNG

DECEMBER IS THE month of holy days and holy nights, a time to express the spirit of love and generosity. It is our remembrance of what is good, true, and beautiful within the human spirit that infuses this month with meaning. The "holy days"—holidays—are a time of spiritual renewal and reflection in many world traditions; a time of gift-giving, as an extension of love, to family, friends, colleagues, and those in need; a time for reflection as the year ends; and a time to renew our wishes for peace on Earth and good will toward everyone.

Whole, Healing Days

It is no coincidence that the root word of whole, health, heal, and holy is *hale* (as in, to be hale and hearty). When we heal, we become whole—we are holy. During the holiday season, it is important to open to the healing forces and natural states of grace that allow us to be hale and hearty once again. The author Madeleine L'Engle reminds us, "The marvellous thing is that this holiness is nothing we can earn. We don't become holy by acquiring merit badges and Brownie points. It has nothing to do with virtue or job descriptions or morality. It is nothing we can *do,* in this do-it-yourself world. It is gift, sheer gift, waiting there to be recognized and received. We do not have to be qualified to be holy. We do not have to be qualified to be whole, or healed." It can be easy to get caught up in the frantic energy of shopping, festivities, and travel this month. Resolve instead to approach the season in a balanced way, to nourish your health and allow your whole self to be present to the holy days and nights.

The Mystic Heart

In the Northern Hemisphere, December is the darkest time of the year, and the month when winter officially begins on the twenty-first with the winter solstice. We await the emergence of gradually increasing light beginning twelve days before Christmas, and we honor the light during Hanukkah, which often falls in December, by lighting the menorah. The African tradition of Kwanzaa celebrates the seven principles of self-determination, and ritualizes respect for the Mystery of light and life itself. In December, we demonstrate our love and open to "the mystic heart" as a way of experiencing more spontaneity, presence, and joy in our lives.

Author Thomas Dreier tells us that much of our creativity and spirituality are mirrors of our internal journey: "The world is a great mirror. It reflects back to you what you are. If you are loving, if you are friendly, if you are helpful, the world will prove loving and friendly and helpful to you. The world is what you are." Notice at this time what the world is mirroring back to you that you could be generating internally, whether what is being reflected is positive or problematic. Our compassionate heart supports our loving and helpful natures, whereas our internal self-doubt or critical nature will mirror back to us some of our struggles, obstacles, and challenges.

All spiritual traditions have a mystical root. *Mysticism* and *mystic* hold the same root word as *mystery,* and in this season when light begins to emerge from darkness, we can explore the mystery of love in our own nature. The spiritual traditions of the world refer to this mystery as "the mystic heart"—a moral capacity within the heart for selfless service and compassionate action. Wayne Teasdale best describes this ecumenical quality of heart in his book *The Mystic Heart:*

> The mystic heart in its maturity reflects the essential
> elements, gifts, and genius of all the traditions of

spiritual wisdom: an actual moral capacity, solidarity with all living beings, deep nonviolence, humility, spiritual practice, mature self-knowledge, simplicity of life, selfless service and compassionate action, and the prophetic voice. These are further refined through a series of capacities that result from the inner journey: openness, presence, listening, being, seeing, spontaneity and joy. . . . All . . . are part of the universal mystical tradition that undergirds the religions and cultures of the world. . . .

A universal spirituality also has a place for various approaches to the transformation from self-interest to other-centeredness, love, compassion, mercy, and kindness. This labor of transformation is the work of the contemplative in all of us, and generously accepting that work permits us to cultivate our own mystic character. The mystic character grows out of humility of heart and simplicity of spirit, a radical openness to what is real.

Take time to reflect and give gratitude for your own mystic heart and how it has expressed itself this year in your work, relationships, health and well-being, and difficult circumstances. Where have you experienced humility of heart and simplicity of spirit this year? This month, express the mystic heart and its transformative power through daily actions of love, compassion, mercy, kindness, and generosity.

Royal Generosity

Generosity of heart is extended cross-culturally through the practice of giving gifts. Every culture of the world gives gifts as offerings of respect, love, good will, and gratitude. There are no exceptions. December is our month of gift-giving, especially to those we love, to those for whom we feel immense gratitude, and to those who are in need or are suffering. Notice the difference in gift-giving when it is motivated by love, generosity, gratitude, and respect rather than by a sense of obligation to participate in a meaningless ritual.

The Irish say that life offers three precious gifts: the gift of life itself; the gift of family; and the gift of friends. The Berber tribes of northern Africa cherish the gifts of shelter, food, family, and health. What gifts do you cherish? What gifts ignite your generosity more than your sense of duty or obligation? The mystical heart within each of us is motivated by "royal generosity"—giving without expecting anything in return. Royal generosity supports the expression of thankful actions. The suras in the Qur'an assert the importance of expressing daily gratitude and thankfulness to God for all that is given or bestowed upon us in our lives. One line from Sura 14 says, "If you are grateful, I will give you more" (14:7). When more is given to us, it can open our hearts to extend generosity of spirit to others in pure-hearted ways. Those who are pure of heart are naturally generous, possessing no agenda or expectation for return. Being pure-hearted is an aspect of the mystical heart, and often is demonstrated more openly through the holidays. Approach your holidays with the spirit of royal generosity that comes from connecting to your own mystical heart as you honor what is whole, or holy, in your life.

The darkness of December and its slow but faithful movement toward the light are crucibles for investigating the mystic heart. There are unlimited ways in which we can connect with our own mystic qualities this month: qualities such as openness, presence, generosity, kindness, and joy. Illuminating December's darkness with candles or colorful lights is an outer action that kindles the reminder of the light of our own inner spirit. Gift-giving offers a wonderful opportunity to express our heartfelt generosity and to delight those who truly matter in our lives. As the year draws to a close, let us recall the many gifts it has brought to us—and that we have brought to the world. Let us end our year of gratitude with appreciation and thanks for all.

DECEMBER BENEFIT OF GRATITUDE-PRACTICE

Did you know that the practices of holding positive emotions and being broad-minded and adaptable in our coping style build upon one another? This leads to increased emotional flexibility and triggers an upward spiral toward enhanced emotional well-being. The heart as an organ responds favorably to positive emotions.

Studies of the physiological effects of positive emotions related to gratitude—namely appreciation and compassion—suggest that changes for the better reliably occur in cardiovascular and immune functioning. In other words, the more we extend gratitude, appreciation, and compassion, the healthier our heart and immune system become.

Reflections

Gratitude is the memory of the heart.

MASSIEU

In contemplative practices of any kind, questions provoke inquiry, reflection, and conscious awareness of what we are learning or what is being revealed to us about our own current inner and outer work.

Notice which of the following questions capture your attention and which are less evocative or interesting to you at this time. Select two or three of the most meaningful questions for you and explore them more deeply.

- December is the month of giving and receiving gifts from family and loved ones. Two kinds of gratitude result: one is the kind we feel when we receive, and the other is what we feel when we give. Notice if it is easier or more difficult for you to receive than it is to give. The mystic heart relishes giving and receiving with equal gratitude and thankfulness, as both are expressions of love—given and received.

- Reflect upon what has been hale, hearty, and whole for you this year. Where has healing occurred in your life and within your nature? Give gratitude for the periods of grace, healing, and wholeness you have experienced.

- Develop the mystic heart and mystic character within your nature: ask or pray for ways to access your moral capacity, develop solidarity with all living things, and commit to nonviolence, selfless service, and humility of spirit.

- What mystical experiences have you had? These are times when you have experienced the dissolution of ego and merged into a sense of profound unity, peace, joy, and love with all that is.

- What have you learned about love this year?

- How do you express generosity of spirit in your life? What acts of royal generosity have you extended this year—to whom and to what? What gifts have you extended to others, and what gifts have you received? In the ritual of gift-giving, what heartfelt and genuine choices have you made that have been pure-hearted?

Practices

Practices are essential for integrating what we are learning. Select two or three of the following practices that most specifically apply to your current experience and would help you the most at this time.

- *Holiday* means "holy day." Take fifteen minutes each day to connect with the sacred Mystery of life and to what you hold and honor as being sacred for you.

- On a daily basis, ask for the grace to let your heart be open and clear.

- Each day this month, take an action that will alleviate suffering in the world or in your family. "Bring light into darkness." Extend an act of kindness or tangibly help those in need through your compassionate actions.

- For the month of December, on a daily basis, extend an act of royal generosity, with which you give, surprise, or delight those who are in need of more joy or less suffering. These may be friends, family members, colleagues, or strangers who could benefit from acts of kindness and generosity. Remember that royal generosity is practiced anonymously, so there is no expectation for a return action in kind.

- Practice this month the art of heartfelt giving and receiving.

- As Thomas Dreier tells us, what we are generating internally is being reflected back to us externally. Notice what is being mirrored back to you on a consistent basis, whether it is positive or problematic. Take actions to make sure that the problematic does not overwhelm the positive.

- This month, write your own poem, invocation, or prayer that evokes comfort and a sense of emotional well-being.

Review and Integration

Gratitude in the Four Quadrants of Life

work   *relationships*

SPIRITUAL GROWTH & DEVELOPING CHARACTER

finances   *health*

Notice what you are grateful for in the four quadrants of your life:

- Work/creative service

- Relationships: friends, colleagues, and family

- Finances and right livelihood

- Health and well-being

The center of the four quadrants represents the place of *developing character* and connecting to your own *spiritual growth* and development. The center is influenced, impacted, and informed by all four quadrants. To help you discover the sources of your gratitude, answer the following tracking questions and see which quadrant or quadrants are emphasized more for you this month.

In looking at the illustration of the Four Quadrants of Life, consider the following questions:

- What are you seeing that is similar to last month's work? What is different, or significantly changing? Review the four quadrants of your life. What is being most activated in either your work, relationships, finances, or health?

- What internal insights and discoveries are you making that have strengthened your character and fostered spiritual growth this month?

- What are you noticing that is new, expanded, or being released in each quadrant of your life this month?

- What are you grateful for in each of your life's quadrants, and how are you expressing your thankfulness?

Blessings, Learnings, Mercies, and Protections

Express your gratitude by reflecting upon:

- The major *Blessings* you have given and received during December.

- The major *Learnings* you have given and received during December.

- The major *Mercies* you have given and received during December.

- The major *Protections* you have given and received during December.

The following questions can help you go deeper in your exploration of these four portals to gratitude.

External Questions

- Who or what has inspired you?

- Who or what is challenging you?

- Who or what is surprising you?

- Who or what is touching or moving you?

Internal Questions

- What is strengthening within my nature?

- What is softening within my nature?

- What is opening within my nature?

- What is deepening within my nature?

Epilogue:
Living in Gratitude—
Where We Have Been and
How We Can Continue

To speak gratitude is courteous and pleasant,
to enact gratitude is generous and noble,
but to live gratitude is Heaven.

JOHANNES A. GAERTNER

Where We Have Been

During the progression of working with the varied chapter themes and their associated reflections and practices, we have discovered and experienced that gratitude is a conscious way of living that keeps the heart open. We have also seen that gratitude is an attitude, or a way of being. Our practice has shown us that gratitude provides strength and solace during dark, challenging times and enhances our lives during light, uplifting times. We now know that it shapes the quality of our experience and positively impacts our well-being, regardless of the difficulties we may face at any given moment. This may well be the reason why Gaertner concluded, "to live in gratitude is Heaven."

Throughout this book, we have explored the impact of gratitude within universal themes of human experience: renewal; love and the heart; compassionate service; mercy and atonement; grace; equanimity; peace; guidance and wisdom; letting be and letting go; the power of grateful seeing; and embracing nature's healing purpose. The quality of our life experience changes when we approach any event or circumstance with gratitude. We become more aware of, and thankful for, the blessings, learnings, mercies, and protections found in the four quadrants of our life—work, relationships, health, and finances—and for the way they shape our spiritual growth and character development.

Through our monthly commitment to giving ourselves the gift of a grateful life, we have accrued its benefits, and we have begun to embody increased health, happiness, compassion, and well-being. With each month's reflections and practices, we have been actively involved in conscious inquiry surrounding our internal and external experiences, which always produces growth, insight, and increased creativity and well-being. Living in gratitude piques our curiosity and increases our desire to learn, reflect, and practice, urging us on in our personal evolution.

The variety of tools and paths that have been presented have shown us new ways to support ourselves in how we will meet and engage more effectively with life's most common experiences. For example, we have examined our relationship to the four life forces we meet daily—love, death, power, and time—and in so doing, perhaps we have observed how important it is to retain childlike curiosity, openness, and honesty. The four-chambered heart has provided a path to keep us aligned with courage, commitment, clarity, and being open to all that life presents. Conscious awareness of what has heart and meaning has inspired us to compassionate service. Our exploration of mercy and atonement has allowed us to open to and be grateful for the gifts of grace and the power of equanimity. Embracing the healing power of nature has helped us cultivate peace and being open to guidance and wisdom, which in turn has enhanced our grateful seeing—one of the most potent gratitude practices. When we shift our perspective to look for what is working in our life and for the good in ourselves and our circumstances, we see the interconnectedness of all things. We open to the great mystery of love and the gift of life itself.

How We Can Continue Living in Gratitude

This book has been designed so that individuals can work with it on their own, in partnership, or in a group. Though it has been constructed to span twelve months, it is not limited to just one year's work. It has been written in a way that anyone can come back to it at any time to strengthen his or her relationship to certain character qualities, or to the perennial wisdom found in each chapter's themes. Whether working individually or in a study group, we can always delve into the themes again and continue to work with one or more in depth, depending on what is calling to be strengthened, supported, or integrated. Each theme, reflection, and practice contains within it lessons that never lose their value. There is always another layer of wisdom and meaning to be integrated on this journey of discovery, whether it is a surprising new connection or an unexpected insight. Returning to the book monthly, seasonally, or at any time of the year, as desired, will empower us to further integrate the practices of gratitude.

The themes contained in this book hold cross-cultural, perennial wisdoms. In working with perennial wisdoms, we become active participants in the shared, cumulative wisdom of the human family, wisdom that will be passed on to future generations. This in itself is a life-changing experience—perhaps it is the ultimate blessing. May we continue to contribute to this deep well of wisdom through living a grateful life, remaining connected to sources of inspiration, challenge, and surprise, and continue to be touched and moved by life's miracles. And may we share with those around us the unlimited healing power of gratitude and its ability to bring out and sustain the good, true, and beautiful within all human beings.

Notes

Introduction

Robert A., Emmons, *Thanks! How the New Science of Gratitude Can Make You Happier* (New York: Houghton Mifflin Company, 2007), 6.

Brother David Steindl-Rast, *Gratefulness, The Heart of Prayer: An Approach to Life in Fullness* (Mahwah, NJ: Paulist Press, 1984), 207.

John O'Donohue, *To Bless the Space Between Us: A Book of Blessings* (New York: Doubleday, 2008), xiii.

Quote from Marge Piercy, as found in: Robert Emmons, *Thanks!* 35.

Ibid., 184.

Robert A., Emmons, and Joanna Hill, *Words of Gratitude for Mind, Body, and Soul.* (West Conshohocken, PA: Templeton Foundation Press, 2001), 87.

Robert A., Emmons, and Michael E. McCullough, eds., *The Psychology of Gratitude* (New York: Oxford University Press, 2004), 158–159.

Ibid., 159.

J. R. Carey et al., "A Test of Positive Reinforcement of Customers," *Journal of Marketing*, Vol. 40, No. 4 (1976): 98–100.

B. Rind and P. Bordia, "Effect of Server's 'Thank You' and Personalization on Restaurant Tipping," *Journal of Applied Social Psychology*, Vol. 25, Issue 9 (1995): 745–751.

Emmons and McCullough, *The Psychology of Gratitude*, 263.

James Hillman, *The Force of Character: And the Lasting Life* (New York: Ballantine Books, 1999), 55.

Geoffrey Sharp, dir., *The Seven Deadly Sins (History Channel)* (United States: A&E Home Video: History Channel, 2009), DVD (2 Discs).

Adapted from Martin Seligman, *Authentic Happiness: Using the New Positive Psychology to Realize Your Potential for Lasting Fulfillment* (New York: Free Press, 2002), 43.

January: Begin Anew

Adapted from Alan W. Jones, *Soul Making: The Desert Way of Spirituality* (New York: HarperCollins, 1989), 132-136.

David L. Cooperrider, ed., et al., "Positive Image, Positive Action The Affirmative Basis of Organizing," in

Appreciative Inquiry: An Emerging Direction for Organization Development (Champaign, IL: Stipes Publishing LLC, 2001), 186.

Adapted from Thomas Banyacya, "The Hopi Message," World Prout Assembly, worldproutassembly.org/archives/2005/12/the_hopi_messag.html.

James Fadiman and Robert Frager, eds., *Essential Sufism* (New York: HarperCollins Publishers, 1997), 82.

Emmons and McCullough, *The Psychology of Gratitude,* 172.

February: Attend to the Heart

Steindl-Rast, *Gratefulness, The Heart of Prayer,* 188.

Ibid., 176.

Myrlie Evers, as cited in *The Wisdom of the Elders,* Robert Flemming, ed. (New York: Ballantine Books, 1997), 210.

Arlie Russell Hochschild and Anne Machung, *The Second Shift* (New York: Penguin Books, 2003), 19.

Corinne McLaughlin and Gordon Davidson, "Dialogues with The Dalai Lama," (2003) visionarylead.org/articles/dalai_lama.htm.

Emmons, *Thanks!,* 45.

Adapted from Ibid., 45–46.

March: Compassionate Service

Alan Jones, John O'Neill, and Diana Landau, *The Seasons of Grace: The Life Giving Practice of Gratitude* (Hoboken, NJ: John Wiley and Sons, Inc., 2003), 12.

Abraham Maslow, *Religions, Values, and Peak Experiences* (New York: Penguin Books, 1994), xii.

Ram Dass and Mirabai Bush, *Compassion in Action: Setting Out On the Path of Service,* 2nd ed. (New York: Bell Tower, 1992), 174.

Aafke E. Komter, *Social Solidarity and the Gift* (Cambridge: Cambridge University Press, 2005), 67.

Brian Boyd, *Vladimir Nabokov: The American Years, Vol. 2,* (Princeton, NJ: Princton University Press, 1991), 154.

Emmons and McCullough, *The Psychology of Gratitude,* 204-210.

April: Mercy and Atonement

D. P. McAdams, *The Redemptive Self: Stories Americans Live By* (New York: Oxford University Press, 2006) as adapted from his article from: *The Psychology of Gratitude.*

Kant information adapted from Emmons, *Thanks!,* 144–146.

Stephen Mitchell, *A Book of Psalms: Selected and Adapted from the Hebrew* (New York: HarperCollins, 1993), 3.

Notes

Karen Armstrong, *The Spiral Staircase: My Climb Out of Darkness* (New York: Anchor Books, a division of Random House, 2005), 272.

Caroline Myss, *Anatomy of the Spirit: The Seven Stages of Power and Healing* (New York: Three Rivers Press, 1996), 84.

Phil Cousineau, *Beyond Forgiveness: Reflections on Atonement* (San Francisco: Jossey-Bass, 2011), 190.

Emmons, *Thanks!*, 12, 44.

Barbara Fredrickson, "The Role of Positive Emotions in Positive Psychology: The Broaden–and–Build Theory of Positive Emotions," *American Psychologist*, Vol. 56, No. 3 (2001): 218–26.

May: The Gift of Grace

Adapted from M. J. Ryan, *Attitudes of Gratitude: How to Give and Receive Joy Every Day of Your Life* (Berkely, CA: Conari Press, 1999), 47.

Thomas Merton as cited in M. J. Ryan, ed., *A Grateful Heart: Daily Blessings for the Evening Meal from the Buddha to the Beatles* (Berkeley, CA: Conari Press, 1994), 52.

Angeles Arrien, *Four-Fold Way: Walking the Paths of the Warrior, Teacher, Healer, and Visionary* (New York: HarperOne, 1993), 114.

Miguel de Unamuno, *Tragic Sense of Life*, trans. J. E. Crawford Flitch (New York: Dover Publications, 1954), 202.

T. B. Kashdan, G. Uswatte, and T. Julian, "Gratitude and Hedonic and Eudaimonic Well-Being in Vietnam War Veterans," Vol. 44 (2006): *Behavior Research and Therapy*, 177–199.

Miyamoto Musashi, "The Earth Book," The Hyoho Niten Ichiryu: Mjer Seiza Nobu Dosokai, hyoho.com/Hyoho4.html.

Emmons, *Thanks!*, 93.

June: The Power of Equanimity

Gregg Krech, *Naikan: Gratitude, Grace, and the Japanese Art of Self-Reflection* (Berkeley, CA: Stone Bridge Press, 2002), 26–27.

Ibid., 31.

Lao Tzu, *Tao Te Ching: A New English Translation,* trans. Stephen Mitchell (New York: Harper Perennial Modern Classics, 2006), 44.

Emmons, *Thanks!*, 12.

Marci Shimoff with Carol Kline, *Happy For No Reason: Seven Steps to Being Happy From the Inside Out* (New York: Free Press, 2008), 244.

July: Embracing Nature

Adapted from Gerald G. May, *The Wisdom of Wilderness: Experiencing the Healing Power of Nature* (New York: HarperCollins, 2006), 23-25.

Notes

Donald G. Kaufman and Cecilia M. Franz, *Biosphere 2000: Protecting our Global Environment,* Third ed. (Dubuque, IA: Kendall Hunt, 2000), 529.

Paul Hawken, *Blessed Unrest: How the Largest Movement in the World Came into Being and Why No One Saw It Coming* (New York: Penguin Group, 2007), 2–4.

Angeles Arrien, *The Second Half of Life: Opening the Eight Gates of Wisdom* (Boulder, CO: Sounds True, 2005), 150.

Richard Louv, *Last Child in the Woods: Saving Our Children From Nature-Deficit Disorder* (Chapel Hill, NC: Algonquin Books, 2008), 35–36.

Lewis Hyde, *The Gift: Creativity and The Artist in the Modern World* (New York: Vintage Books, 1983), 148.

August: Cultivating Peace

Archbishop of York (Dr. Sentamu), "Prayers for Peace in the Middle East with the Archbishop: A Selection of the Prayers used by Dr. Sentamu in Leading Public Intersessions in York Minster Every Hour During the Day of the Week, throughout his Vigil: 'Oh God You Are Peace: Islamic Prayer'", Diocese of York, England, archbishopofyork.org/263?q=prayers+for+peace+in+middle+east. Reprinted with permission from the Archbishop of York, England.

Quaker queries as cited in Jay Marshall, *Thanking and Blessing–The Sacred Art: Spiritual Vitality Through Gratefulness* (Woodstock, VT: Skylight Paths Publishing, 2007), 135–136.

Louise Diamond, *The Peace Book: 108 Simple Ways to Create a More Peaceful World* (Berkeley, CA: Conari Press, 2001), 122.

Ibid., 122.

September: Opening to Guidance and Wisdom

Roger Walsh, *Essential Spirituality: The Seven Central Practices to Awaken Heart and Mind* (New York: John Wiley and Sons, 1999), 14.

Stephen R. Covey, *The Seven Habits of Highly Effective People* (New York: Simon and Schuster, 1989).

Ibid., 109–110.

Dr. Darren R. Weissman, *The Power of Infinite Love and Gratitude: An Evolutionary Journey to Awakening Your Spirit* (Carlsbad, CA: Hay House, 2005), 158.

Dr. William Stewart, *Deep Medicine: Harnessing the Source of Your Healing Power* (Oakland, CA: New Harbinger, 2009), xii–xiii.

Mike Robbins, *Focus on the Good Stuff: The Power of Appreciation* (San Francisco: Jossey-Bass, 2007), 15.

Adapted from John F. Demartini, *Count Your Blessings: The Healing Power of Gratitude and Love* (Carlsbad, CA: Hay House, 2006), 111–12.

October: Letting Be and Letting Go

Matthew Fox, *The A.W.E. Project: Reinventing Education, Reinventing the Human* (Kelowna, BC, Canada: CopperHouse, 2006), 118–119.

Peter Block, *Answer to How is Yes: Acting on What Matters* (San Francisco: Berrett-Koehler Publishers, 2002), 182.

Dr. William Glasser, as cited in Shimoff and Kline, *Happy For No Reason,* 281–82.

November: Grateful Seeing

"Address of John Paul II to the Pilgrims Who had Come to Rome for the Beatification of Mother Teresa," The Holy See, vatican.va/holy_father/john_paul_ii/speeches/2003/october/documents/hf_jp-ii_spe_20031020_pilgrims-mother-teresa_en.html.

Fred Luskin, *Forgive for Good: A Proven Prescription for Health and Happiness* (San Francisco: HarperSanFrancisco, 2002), 116.

Emmet Fox, *The Sermon on the Mount: The Key to Success in Life* (New York: HarperCollins, 1966), 113–114.

Adapted from Dacher Keltner, *Born to be Good: The Science of a Meaningful Life* (New York: W. W. Norton and Company, 2009). 3–6.

Emmons and McCullough, *The Psychology of Gratitude,* 278.

December: The Mystic Heart

Maggie Oman, ed., *Prayers for Healing: 365 Blessings, Poems, and Meditations from Around the World* (Berkeley, CA: Conari Press, 1997), 252.

Wayne Teasdale, *The Mystic Heart: Discovering a Universal Spirituality in the World's Religions* (Novato, CA: New World Library, 1999), 243–245.

Emmons and McCullough, *Psychology of Gratitude,* 156.

Bibliography

"Ancient Prayer of Thanksgiving of the Haudenosaunee
Nation."onondaganation.org

Anonymous. "May We Appreciate and Remember: A Buddhist
Blessing."

Appleton, George, ed. *The Oxford Book of Prayer.* New York:
Oxford University Press, 2009.

Archbishop of York, (Dr. Sentamu). "Prayers for Peace in
the Middle East with the Archbishop: A Selection of
the Prayers Used by Dr. Sentamu in Leading Public
Intersessions in York Minster Every Hour During the
Day of the Week, Throughout His Vigil: 'Oh God You
Are Peace: Islamic Prayer'." Diocese of York, England,
archbishopofyork.org/263?q=prayers+for+peace+in+
middle+east.

Armstrong, Karen. "Charter for Compassion." http://
charterforcompassion.org.

———. *The Spiral Staircase: My Climb Out of Darkness*. New York: Anchor Books, 2005.

———. *Twelve Steps to a Compassionate Life*. New York: Alfred A. Knopf, 2010.

Arrien, Angeles. *The Four-Fold Way: Walking the Paths of the Warrior, Teacher, Healer and Visionary*. New York: HarperOne, 1993.

———. *The Second Half of Life: Opening the Eight Gates of Wisdom*. Boulder, CO: Sounds True, 2005.

Augustine, Saint. *St. Augustine*. Vol. 18, Great Books of the Western World. Chicago, IL: Encyclopedia Britannica, 1990.

Bailey, Pearl. "Daily Celebrations: Life Is a Celebration of Passionate Colors—Today in History and More . . . To Motivate, Educate and Inspire." coolpup.com, dailycelebrations.com/032903.htm.

Ban Brethnak, Sarah. *Simple Abundance: A Daybook of Comfort and Joy*. New York: Warner Books, 1995.

Banyacya, Thomas. "The Hopi Message." World Prout Assembly, worldproutassembly.org/archives/2005/12/the_hopi_messag.html.

"Be Thankful: Living with Gratitude." bethankful.com/quotes.htm.

Blackburn, Simon. *Lust: The Seven Deadly Sins*. New York: Oxford University Press, 2006.

Bibliography

Block, Peter. *The Answer to How Is Yes: Acting on What Matters.* San Francisco: Berrett-Koehler Publishers, 2002.

————. *Community: A Structure for Belonging.* San Francisco: Berrett-Koehler Publishers, 2008.

Boyd, Brian. *Vladimir Nabokov: The American Years.* Vol. 2. Princeton, NJ: Princeton University Press, 1991.

Butash, Adrian. *Bless This Food: Ancient and Contemporary Graces from around the World.* Novato, CA: New World Library, 2007.

Carey, J. R., S. H. Clicque, B. A. Leighton, and F. Milton. "A Test of Positive Reinforcement of Customers." *Journal of Marketing,* Vol. 40, no. 4 (1976): 98–100.

Chapman, Gary. *The Five Love Languages: How to Express Heartfelt Commitment to Your Mate.* Chicago: Northfield Publishing, 1995.

Cook, John, Steve Deger, and Leslie Gibson, eds. *The Book of Positive Quotations.* Minneapolis, MN: Fairview Press, 1997.

Cooperrider, David L., Peter F. Sorensen Jr., Therese F. Yaeger, and Diana Whitney, eds. "Positive Image, Positive Action: The Affirmative Basis of Organizing." In *Appreciative Inquiry: An Emerging Direction for Organization Development.* Champaign, IL: Stipes Publishing LLC, 2001.

Cousineau, Phil. *Beyond Forgiveness: Reflections on Atonement.* San Francisco: Jossey-Bass, 2011.

Covey, Stephen R. *The Seven Habits of Highly Effective People*. New York: Simon and Schuster, 1989.

Croft, Jack, and Prevention Magazine Editors, eds. *The Doctors Book of Home Remedies for Men*. New York: Bantam Books, 2000.

Dass, Ram, and Mirabai Bush. *Compassion in Action: Setting Out on the Path of Service*. 2nd ed. New York: Bell Tower, 1992.

de Unamuno, Miguel. *Tragic Sense of Life*. Translated by J. E. Crawford Flitch. New York: Dover Publications, 1954.

Demartini, John F. *Count Your Blessings: The Healing Power of Gratitude and Love*. Carlsbad, CA: Hay House, 2006.

Diamond, Louise. *The Peace Book: 108 Simple Ways to Create a More Peaceful World*. Berkeley, CA: Conari Press, 2001.

Dickinson, Emily. *The Complete Poems of Emily Dickinson*. Edited by Thomas H. Johnson. New York: Little, Brown, 1960.

Dyson, Michael Eric. *Pride: The Seven Deadly Sins*. New York: Oxford University Press, 2006.

Einstein, Albert. "The World as I See It." American Public Media, speakingoffaith.publicradio.org/programs/einsteinsethics/einstein-theworldasiseeit.shtml.

———. *The World as I See It*. San Diego, CA: The Book Tree, 2007.

Emerson, Ralph Waldo. "Thanksgiving." worldprayers.org/
frameit.cgi?/archive/prayers/celebrations/for_each_new_
morning_with.html.

Emmons, Robert A. *Thanks! How the New Science of Gratitude
Can Make You Happier.* New York: Houghton Mifflin,
2007.

Emmons, Robert A., and Joanna Hill. *Words of Gratitude
for Mind, Body, and Soul.* West Conshohocken, PA:
Templeton Foundation Press, 2001.

Emmons, Robert A., and Michael E. McCullough, eds.
The Psychology of Gratitude, Series in Affective Science.
New York: Oxford University Press, 2004.

Epstein, Joseph. *Envy: The Seven Deadly Sins.* New York:
Oxford University Press, 2006.

Erikson, Erik. *Childhood and Society.* 2nd ed. New York:
W. W. Norton & Company, 1963.

Evers-Williams, Myrlie, and Melinda Blau. *Watch Me Fly:
What I Learned on the Way to Becoming the Woman I Was
Meant to Be.* New York: NY: Little, Brown, 1999.

Fadiman, James, and Robert Frager, eds. *Essential Sufism.* New
York: HarperCollins Publishers, 1997.

"First Psalm." In *The Holy Bible.* New York: Oxford University
Press, 2000.

Flemming, Robert, ed. *The Wisdom of the Elders.* New York:
Ballantine Books, 1997.

Bibliography

Fox, Emmet. *The Sermon on the Mount: The Key to Success in Life*. New York: HarperCollins Publishers, Inc., 1966.

Fox, Matthew. *The A.W.E. Project: Reinventing Education, Reinventing the Human*. Kelowna, BC, Canada: CopperHouse, 2006.

Fox, Matthew, and Rupert Sheldrake. *Natural Grace*. New York: Doubleday Image, 1996.

Fredrickson, Barbara L. "The Role of Positive Emotions in Positive Psychology: The Broaden-and-Build Theory of Positive Emotions." *American Psychologist*. Vol. 56, no. 3 (2001): 218-26.

Frost, Robert. *A Boy's Will*. New York: Henry Holt, 1915.

Gallagher, Winifred. *Spiritual Genius: Ten Masters and the Quest for Meaning*. New York: Random House, 2002.

Gerzon, Mark. "Mediator's Foundation." mediatorsfoundation.org.

Gibran, Kahlil. *The Prophet*. London: Wordsworth Editions, Ltd., 1996.

Glasser, Dr. William. *Every Student Can Succeed*. Chula Vista, CA: Black Forest Press, 2000.

"Global Impact: Assuring Help for People in Need." charity.org.

Gottman, John M., and Nan Silver. *The Seven Principles for Making Marriage Work: A Practical Guide from the Country's Foremost Relationship Expert*. New York: Three Rivers Press, 1999.

Bibliography

Graham, Mark E. *Sustainable Agriculture: A Christian Ethic of Gratitude.* Eugene, OR: Wipf and Stock Publishers, 2009.

Hammarskjold, Dag. *Markings.* Translated by Leif Sjoberg and W. H. Auden. New York: Ballantine Books, 1964.

Hanh, Thich Nhat, and the Monks and Nuns of Plum Village. *Plum Village Chanting and Recitation Book.* Berkeley, CA: Parallax Press, 2000.

Hawken, Paul. *Blessed Unrest: How the Largest Movement in the World Came into Being and Why No One Saw It Coming.* New York: Penguin Group, 2007.

Hay, Louise L. *Gratitude: A Way of Life.* Carlsbad, CA: Hay House, 1996.

Herbert, George. "The Flower." en.wikiquote.org/wiki/George_Herbert.

Hillman, James. *The Force of Character: And the Lasting Life.* New York: Ballantine Books, 1999.

Hochschild, Arlie Russell, and Anne Machung. *The Second Shift.* New York: Penguin, 2003.

The Holy Bible. New York: Oxford University Press, 2000.

Hyde, Lewis. *The Gift: Creativity and the Artist in the Modern World.* New York: Vintage Books, 1983.

"An Islamic Prayer for Peace." Cornell University: Cornell United Religious Work, curw.cornell.edu/prayer4.html.

Jeffers, Robinson. *The Selected Poetry of Robinson Jeffers*. Edited by Tim Hunt. Stanford, CA: Stanford University Press, 2001.

"Job, 12:8". In *The Holy Bible*. New York: Oxford University Press, 2000.

"John, 1:16". In *The Holy Bible*. New York: Oxford University Press, 2000.

John Paul II, H. H. Pope "Address of John Paul II to the Pilgrims Who Had Come to Rome for the Beatification of Mother Teresa." The Holy See, vatican.va/holy_father/ john_paul_ii/speeches/ 2003/october/documents/ hf_jp-ii_spe_20031020_pilgrims-mother-teresa-en.html.

Jones, Alan, John O'Neill, and Diana Landau. *The Seasons of Grace: The Life-Giving Practice of Gratitude*. Hoboken, NJ: John Wiley and Sons, 2003.

Jones, Alan W. *Soul Making: The Desert Way of Spirituality*. New York: HarperCollins Publishers, 1989.

Jung, C. G. *Memories, Dreams, Reflections*. Edited by Aniela Jaffe. New York: Vintage, 1989.

Kashdan, T. B., G. Uswatte, and T. Julian. "Gratitude and Hedonic and Eudaimonic Well-being in Vietnam War Veterans." *Behavior Research and Therapy*, Vol. 44, (2006): 177-99.

Kaufman, Donald G., and Cecilia M. Franz. *Biosphere 2000: Protecting Our Global Environment*. 3rd ed. Dubuque, IA: Kendall Hunt Publishing Co., 2000.

Bibliography

Keltner, Dacher. *Born to Be Good: The Science of a Meaningful Life*. New York: W. W. Norton and Company, 2009.

Keltner, Dacher, Jason Mars, and Jeremy Adam Smith, eds. *The Compassion Instinct: The Science of Human Goodness*. New York: W. W. Norton and Company, 2010.

Komter, Aafke E. *Social Solidarity and the Gift*. Cambridge, UK: Cambridge University Press, 2005.

Kornfield, Jack. *The Art of Forgiveness, Lovingkindness, and Peace*. New York: Bantam Books, 2002.

Krech, Gregg. *Naikan: Gratitude, Grace, and the Japanese Art of Self-Reflection*. Berkeley, CA: Stone Bridge Press, 2002.

Lama, Dalai. *The Dalai Lama's Book of Wisdom*. London: HarperThorsons Publishers, 2000.

———. *The Dalai Lama's Little Book of Inner Peace: The Essential Life and Teachings*. Newburyport, MA: Hampton Roads Publishing, 2009.

Leddy, Mary Jo. *Radical Gratitude*. Maryknoll, NY: Orbis Books, 2002.

Lorie, Peter, and Manuela Dunn Mascetti, eds. *The Quotable Spirit: A Treasury of Religious Quotations from Ancient Times to the 20th Century*. Edison, NJ: Castle Books, 1996.

Louv, Richard. *Last Child in the Woods: Saving Our Children from Nature-Deficit Disorder*. Chapel Hill, NC: Algonquin Books, 2008.

Bibliography

Luskin, Fred. *Forgive for Good: A Proven Prescription for Health and Happiness.* San Francisco: HarperSanFrancisco, 2002.

Marshall, PhD, Jay. *Thanking and Blessing–the Sacred Art: Spiritual Vitality through Gratefulness.* Woodstock, VT: Skylight Paths Publishing, 2007.

Maslow, Abraham. *Religions, Values, and Peak Experiences.* New York: Penguin, 1994.

May, Gerald G. *The Wisdom of Wilderness: Experiencing the Healing Power of Nature.* New York: HarperCollins, 2006.

McAdams, Dan P. *The Redemptive Self: Stories Americans Live By.* New York: Oxford University Press, 2006.

McLaughlin, Corinne, and Gordon Davidson. "Dialogues with The Dalai Lama." (2003) visionarylead.org/articles/dalai_lama.htm.

Mitchell, Stephen. *A Book of Psalms: Selected and Adapted from the Hebrew.* New York: HarperCollins, 1993.

Montaldo, Jonathan, and Robert G. Toth, eds. *Bridges to Contemplative Living with Thomas Merton: Entering the School of Your Experience.* Indiana: Ave Maria Press, Notre Dame, IN: 2006.

Moore, Thomas. *The Soul's Religion: Cultivating a Profoundly Spiritual Way of Life.* New York: HarperCollins, 2003.

Musashi, Miyamoto. *The Book of Five Rings.* Translated by Thomas Cleary. Boston: Shambhala Publications, Inc, 1993.

Bibliography

———. "The Earth Book." The Hyoho Niten Ichiryu: Mjer Seiza Nobu Dosokai, hyoho.com/Hyoho4.html.

Myss, Caroline. *Anatomy of the Spirit: The Seven Stages of Power and Healing.* New York: Three Rivers Press, 1996.

Nabokov, Vladimir. *Speak Memory.* New York: Everyman's Library: Alfred A. Knopf, 1999.

Nayyar, Pyarelal. *Mahatma Gandhi: The Last Phase.* Vol. 2. Ahmedabad, India: Navajivan Publishing House, 1958.

"Nebraska Mediation Association." nemediation.org.

Needleman, Jacob. *The American Soul: Rediscovering the Wisdom of the Founders.* New York: Jeremy P. Tarcher/ Putnam, 2003.

Niebuhr, Reinhold. "The Serenity Prayer." Alcoholics Anonymous (AA History.com), aahistory.com/prayer.html.

O'Donohue, John. *Eternal Echoes: Exploring Our Yearning to Belong.* New York: Cliff Street Books, 1999.

———. *To Bless the Space between Us: A Book of Blessings.* New York: Doubleday, 2008.

O'Neill, Patrick. "Extraordinary Conversations." extraordinaryconversations.com.

Oman, Maggie, ed. *Prayers for Healing: 365 Blessings, Poems, and Meditations from Around the World.* Berkeley, CA: Conari Press, 1997.

Oman Shannon, Maggie ed. *Prayers for Hope and Comfort: Reflections, Meditations, and Inpirations.* San Francisco: Conari Press, 2008.

"Outward Bound." outwardbound.org.

Porras, Jerry, Stewart Emery, and Mark Thompson. *Success Built to Last: Creating a Life That Matters.* Upper Saddle River, NJ: Wharton School Publishing, 2007.

Prose, Francine. *Gluttony: The Seven Deadly Sins.* New York: Oxford University Press, 2006.

Richo, David. *The Sacred Heart of the World: Restoring Mystical Devotion to Our Spiritual Life.* Mahwah, NJ: Paulist Press, 2007.

————. *When Love Meets Fear: Becoming Defense-Less and Resource-Full.* Mahwah: Paulist Press, 1997.

————. ed. *Wisdom's Way: Quotations for Contemplation.* Berkeley, CA: Human Development Books, 2008.

Rind, B., and P. Bordia. "Effect of Server's 'Thank You' and Personalization on Restaurant Tipping." *Journal of Applied Social Psychology,* Vol. 25; Issue 9 (1995): 745–51.

Robbins, Mike. *Be Yourself, Everyone Else Is Already Taken: Transform Your Life with the Power of Authenticity.* San Francisco: Jossey-Bass, 2009.

————. *Focus on the Good Stuff: The Power of Appreciation.* San Francisco, CA: Jossey-Bass, a Wiley imprint, 2007.

Robinson, B. A. "Summer Solstice Celebrations: Ancient and Modern." Religious Tolerance: Ontario Consultants on Religious Tolerance, religioustolerance.org/summer_solstice.htm.

Rosenberg, Marshall. *Non-Violent Communication: A Language of Life.* 2nd ed. Encinitas, CA: Puddledancer Press, 2003.

Roth, John K. *International Encyclopedia of Ethics.* London: Routledge, 1995.

Rumi, Jalal al-Din. *The Essential Rumi.* Translated by Coleman Barks. Edison, NJ: Castle Books, 1997.

Ryan, M. J. *Attitudes of Gratitude: How to Give and Receive Joy Every Day of Your Life.* Berkeley, CA: Conari Press, 1999.

————. ed. *A Grateful Heart: Daily Blessings for the Evening Meal from Buddha to the Beatles.* Berkeley, CA: Conari Press, 1994.

Schechter, Howard. *Jupiter's Rings: Balance from the Inside Out.* Ashland, OR: White Cloud Press, 2002.

Seligman, Martin. *Authentic Happiness: Using the New Positive Psychology to Realize Your Potential for Lasting Fulfillment.* New York: Free Press, 2002.

————. *What You Can Change and What You Can't: The Complete Guide to Successful Self-Improvement.* New York: Vintage Books, Random House Group, 2007.

Bibliography

Sharp, Geoffrey: Director *The Seven Deadly Sins (History Channel)*. United States: A&E Home Video: History Channel, 2009. DVD (2 Discs).

Shimoff, Marci, with Carol Kline. *Happy for No Reason: Seven Steps to Being Happy from the Inside Out.* New York: Free Press, 2008.

Shoshanna, Brenda. *365 Ways to Give Thanks: One for Every Day of the Year.* New York: Citadel: Carol Publishing Group Edition, 2000.

Snyder, C. R., and Shane J. Lopez, eds. *Oxford Handbook of Positive Psychology.* 2nd ed., Oxford Library of Psychology. New York: Oxford University Press, 2009.

Steindl-Rast, Brother David. *Gratefulness, the Heart of Prayer: An Approach to Life in Fullness.* Mahwah, NJ: Paulist Press, 1984.

Stevenson, Robert Louis. *Prayers Written at Vailima: For Success.* South Australia: The University of Adelaide Library: ebooks@adelaide.

Stewart, Dr. William B. *Deep Medicine: Harnessing the Source of Your Healing Power.* Oakland, CA: New Harbinger Publications, 2009.

Straub, Gail. *The Rhythm of Compassion: Caring for Self, Connecting with Society.* Boston: Tuttle Publishing, 2000.

Tagore, Taz. *Seasons of Thanks: Graces and Blessings for Every Home.* New York: Stewart, Tabori and Chang, an imprint of Abrams, 2005.

Bibliography

Teasdale, Wayne. *The Mystic Heart: Discovering a Universal Spirituality in the World's Religions*. Novato, CA: New World Library, 1999.

Thurman, Robert A. F. *Anger: The Seven Deadly Sins*. New York: Oxford University Press, 2006.

Tickle, Phyllis. *Greed: The Seven Deadly Sins*. New York: Oxford University Press, 2006.

Tzu, Lao. *Tao Te Ching: A New English Version*. Translated by Stephen Mitchell. New York: Harper Perennial Modern Classics, 2006.

Uhlein, Gabrielle. *Meditations with Hildegard of Bingen*. Rochester, VT: Bear and Company, 1983.

Walsh, MD, PhD, Roger. *Essential Spirituality: The Seven Central Practices to Awaken Heart and Mind*. New York: John Wiley and Sons, 1999.

Wasserstein, Wendy. *Sloth: The Seven Deadly Sins*. New York: Oxford University Press, 2006.

Weissman, Dr. Darren R. *The Power of Infinite Love and Gratitude: An Evolutionary Journey to Awakening Your Spirit*. Carlsbad, CA: Hay House, Inc., 2005.

"Wiser Earth: The Social Network for Sustainability." wiserearth.com.

Worthington Jr., Everett L. *Forgiving and Reconciling: Bridges to Wholeness and Hope*. Downers Grove, IL: InterVarsity Press, 2003.

Reader's Guide

Discussion Questions

1. What are you learning from the four themes of soul-making and what new beginnings are you making this month?

- Love: Your desire for union and meaningful connection
- Death: Your ability to release, let go, and surrender
- Power: Your ability to sustain right use of power and stay connected to your heart and your integrity
- Time: Your relationship to time reveals your capacity to trust that whatever is present each day, you can handle; otherwise it would not be there. The surprising or unexpected happenings of each day reveal your attachments and teach you about your ability or inability to remain flexible.

2. Are you attending daily to the four-chambered heart?
Keep these four questions in mind as you work with your heart practice:

- In what areas of your life do you feel half-hearted rather than full-hearted?
- When do you feel weak-hearted rather than strong-hearted?
- When do you feel closed-hearted when you could be open-hearted?
- In what ways are you confused or doubting rather than clear-hearted?

3. What wise actions of thankfulness and generosity do you want to extend to yourself and others this month? Where does compassionate service appear in your life?

The practice of gratitude keeps the heart open. Discernment is wisdom's way to ensure we take appropriate and wise action to connect with what has heart and meaning for us. Compassionate action implements heartfelt service with wise action. What areas of your life are you involved with compassionate service?

4. What self-forgiveness work is revealing itself as something you need to address at this time?

As you consider this, ask yourself:

- What reparation work, amends, or act of mercy will enable you to forgive yourself and others?
- What is it that you are not yet willing to forgive? Can you forgive yourself for that? What states of ingratitude still require vigilence for you?

5. What ancestors have impacted or inspired your own interests and journey?

- Think about what ancestral stories, songs, and rituals are present in your family or have been passed along from generation to generation.
- In what ways will your journey and life's work impact future generations? How will you be remembered as an ancestor?
- Create a list of ways you *already* honor those who have gone before you, and add ideas for new ways you could express gratitude to your ancestors.

6. Do you make time to be quiet each day?

Spending time in silence cultivates and strengthens our connection to the sense of peacefulness and acceptance that is available to us in states of equanimity. Set aside a half hour each day to sit or walk in silence. Notice what is revealed to you in the silence—especially the solace and peaceful moments it offers you.

7. What part does nature play in your day-to-day life?

Spend a full hour outdoors every day to increase your health and well-being. As creatures of nature, we need natural light and air to support our health. The more we spend quality time in nature, the more we get in touch with our internal nature.

8. When have you practiced nonviolence in your life?

Our acts of courage often reveal to us our sense of justice or integrity—the urge to do the right thing, even when others may not do the same. It is our courage and integrity that dispel our conflict-avoidant or appeasing patterns. When we notice signs of weak-heartedness we know we have inner work to do with regards to courage and integrity. Ask yourself what circumstances or people are calling for you to be courageous at this time.

9. Do you express gratitude to yourself for your efforts and good intentions?

At the end of each day, acknowledge to yourself the excellent work and creativity you have extended to your family and coworkers. Notice where you have genuinely acknowledged the particular gifts, talents, skills, and character qualities you have observed in others. Whatever and whomever we appreciate, including ourselves, appreciates (increases in value), amplifies, or expands.

10. In what ways are you a social architect? How do you bring out or enhance what matters most to people in families, organizations, and communities?

A social architect evokes the gifts and talents of others, supports the manifestation of an individual's longings, and embodies the ability to "let be and let go." Who brings out the best in you? These are the social architects in your life.

11. How are you shifting your perspective from focusing on what's not working to developing "grateful seeing"?

Try looking first for what *is* working and what is good in your life. Grateful seeing does not ignore what is problematic or not working; it begins first with what is working in one's life—before beginning to problem solve.

12. How are you contributing to creating a better world?
Take an action each day this month that will alleviate suffering in the world or in your family. "Bring light into darkness." Extend an act of kindness or tangibly help those in need through your compassionate actions. In what ways are you developing "the mysitic heart" or involved in ways of practicing the golden rule—"Doing unto others as you would have done to you?"

About the Author

Angeles Arrien, PhD (1940–2014) received her master's degree from the University of California at Berkeley, and her doctorate from the California Institute for Integral Studies. Dr. Arrien's teachings bridge the disciplines of anthropology, psychology, and comparative religion, while focusing on universal beliefs shared by humanity. She lectured and led workshops internationally on cultural anthropology and transpersonal psychology at colleges, corporate settings, and personal growth facilities. Her books include *The Four-Fold Way*, *The Second Half of Life*, and *Living in Gratitude*, and her audio-learning programs include *Gratitude*, *Gathering Medicine*, and more.

intergenerational and indigenous educational bridging projects have positively impacted youth and elders in more than twenty countries.

Angeles is the author of six books, including *The Four-Fold Way*, *Signs of Life* (winner of the 1993 Benjamin Franklin Award), and *The Second Half of Life* (winner of the 2007 Nautilus Award for Best Book on Aging). Her books have been translated into thirteen languages, and she has received three honorary doctorate degrees in recognition of her work.

You can find out more about Angeles at her website: angelesarrien.com.

About Sounds True

Sounds True is a multimedia publisher whose mission is to inspire and support personal transformation and spiritual awakening. Founded in 1985 and located in Boulder, Colorado, we work with many of the leading spiritual teachers, thinkers, healers, and visionary artists of our time. We strive with every title to preserve the essential "living wisdom" of the author or artist. It is our goal to create products that not only provide information to a reader or listener, but that also embody the quality of a wisdom transmission.

For those seeking genuine transformation, Sounds True is your trusted partner. At SoundsTrue.com you will find a wealth of free resources to support your journey, including exclusive weekly audio interviews, free downloads, interactive learning tools, and other special savings on all our titles.

To learn more, please visit SoundsTrue.com/freegifts or call us toll free at 800-333-9185.

SOUNDS TRUE
many voices, one journey